# Magickal Mermaids
## & Water Creatures

# Magickal Mermaids & Water Creatures

---

## D.J. CONWAY

### Foreword by Skye Alexander

**WEISER BOOKS**

This edition first published in 2019 by Weiser Books, an imprint of

Red Wheel/Weiser, LLC
With offices at:
65 Parker Street, Suite 7
Newburyport, MA 01950
*www.redwheelweiser.com*

ISBN: 978-1-57863-683-9

Library of Congress Cataloging-in-Publication Data available upon request.

Cover design by Kathryn Sky-Peck and Kasandra Cook
Cover photograph © Yuri Arcurs / Getty Images
Interior photos/images by Shutterstock
Interior by Kathryn Sky-Peck
Typeset in Adobe Caslon Pro and Incognito

Printed in the United States of America
IBI
10 9 8 7 6 5 4 3 2 1

# Contents

## Part Three
## Connections, Warnings, and Power

## Part Four
## Rituals for Mermaids and Water Folk

# Foreword

Why do mermaids fascinate us? Why has their allure lasted for millennia, in cultures around the world, and grown stronger now than ever before? Yes, mermaids are incredibly beautiful and their exquisite singing reputedly sends men into throes of ecstasy. But more than that, it's their mysterious magickal powers that intrigue us. They govern the weather, foresee the future, and live forever. They can transform themselves from entities who occupy the watery depths into humanlike creatures who walk among us on dry land. Today, as in ancient times, we're entranced by the mermaids' mystique. Do these beguiling beings really exist? Where can we meet them? What can we learn from them?

In *Magickal Mermaids and Water Creatures,* noted author, tarot deck designer, magick worker, and respected spiritual teacher D.J. Conway provides answers to these and many more questions. Here Conway shares mermaid legends from the British Isles and Europe, from the Middle and Far East, from Africa and the Americas. Some of the earliest creation myths talk about an aquatic female who "birthed" life on earth by mingling the salt and fresh waters. Archaeologists have discovered paintings and figurines of mer-folk dating back to the ancient civilizations of Babylonia, Persia, and Mesopotamia—proof that mermaids (or at least our beliefs about them) have been around since antiquity.

Undoubtedly you're familiar with mermaids, but you may not realize that mermen reside in the world's waterways too. And as you'll soon see, mer-folk don't always appear as the hybrid creatures we usually think of, with human torsos and fishy tails—some sport snake-like appendages, dolphin parts, or sealskins. They can even shed their tails to come ashore, where they look just like people except for the webs of skin between their fingers and toes. Some (like the Starbucks mermaid) have two tails or a split tail that allows them to mate with humans—and the offspring of these unions are unique to say the least!

Not only do mer-folk populate the seven seas, they also make their homes in rivers and streams, lakes and marshes, even wells and fountains. In *Magickal Mermaids and Water Creatures*, you'll meet a menagerie of mer-folk, including the Merry Maids of Cornwall who'll grant three wishes if you capture them; the Mediterranean sea nymphs known as Nereids who ride the waves on the backs of porpoises; the dangerous Lorelei who live in Germany's Rhine River where their singing mesmerizes sailors and lures them to watery graves. You'll also learn about odd and mysterious aquatic creatures with ties to mermaids, such as Tarroo-Ushtey, a wild bull that lives in the ocean, and the hippocampus, a half-horse half-fish that legends say pulled the chariot of the Greek sea god Poseidon. Conway describes where they live (in underwater palaces made of gold and jewels collected from sunken ships), what they eat, and what they do for entertainment. She also explains how these amazing creatures can assist or harm you—they're capricious, she warns, and they don't embrace the same codes of ethics humans do, nor do they make strong emotional attachments to mortals. And woe be to earthlings who offend the mer-folk!

Would you like to meet a mermaid? According to folklore, mermaids can grant wishes, increase your psychic powers, lead you to treasure, offer protection, and provide healing. They can also teach you the secrets of water magick. In *Magickal Mermaids and Water Creatures*, Conway shares her extensive knowledge of spellcraft and invites you to join your skills with those of the mer-folk, using shells, gemstones, plants, and other accouterments to generate outcomes you desire. She teaches you how to befriend mermaids through meditations and rituals, by building stone symbols near a body of water, and offering gifts of gemstones or jewelry. You'll know when a mermaid is talking to you because she'll speak in words you don't ordinarily use or she'll express opinions that may be different from those you normally hold.

You may wonder why, if mermaids are so prevalent and have been with us since the beginning of time, we haven't found tangible evidence of them. Countless people claim to have seen these mysterious beings, but scant physical proof exists. That's because mermaids now live in the astral realm, Conway tells us. Occasionally, though, they let us glimpse them frolicking on the waves or combing their hair by the shoreline—and we're delighted by these special visitations. Those who've had the rare privilege of spotting a mermaid never forget the experience.

Perhaps the reason we love mermaids today more than ever is that we really need them now. At this crucial time when pollution and climate change endanger all creatures on Earth—especially the aquatic ones—we must expand our understanding and appreciation for our planet's waters and marine life. Our own lives depend on it. Mermaids can serve as our teachers.

—Skye Alexander,
author of *Mermaids: The Myths, Legends, & Lore*
and *Magickal Astrology*

# PART I

# Introduction to Mermaids and Water Creatures

# CHAPTER 1

# Secret Powers
of the Mermaids

Mermaids—the mystical word conjures up age-old images of sea sirens, beautiful half-fish women who live along the shores of all the major oceans of the world. Their relationship with humans has always been one of mixed emotions and reactions on both sides. Perhaps this is because humans are closer in physical form to the mer-folk than to any other mystical creature. Perhaps it is because we expect a similar-looking species to think and act as we do.

Are mermaids real? Just because a number of different creatures can transport themselves quickly and easily between the astral realms and this world does not mean they are illusions and do not exist. It simply means humans must be much more aware of their surroundings if they wish to see these beings. We tend to be aware of the big picture and forget to look at the small, lovely details in life.

It is very difficult to explain about the Earth and astral realm issue with the mermaids and other water creatures, because the old tales speak of them as actually having been in this world. However, at some time this species and many others decided to move completely to the astral realm for safety. The mermaids, other beings, and their habitats and civilizations are now entirely found in the astral realm, although they have the ability to visit the physical plane whenever they wish. I have seen only one mermaid personally, and because I had binoculars, there was no doubt what the being was. Clearly, I saw the long pale flash of arms and head as the mermaid leaped and played in the waves. Each time she went beneath the water, her iridescent fish tail was very visible. In her last dive, she smacked the ocean waters with her tail, as if laughing at my astonishment. However, physical sightings are rare in modern times. Therefore, most of the information I entered into this book is a combination of very old tales and personal experience in spiritual interactions and deep meditations. Rather than sound like a dull professor reading from a textbook and reiterate this throughout the book, I have chosen to write as if these occurrences and meetings are ordinary physical events.

Mermaids are not seals, nor are they manatees. No human could mistake either of these physical, earthly water creatures for a half-human mermaid with bare breasts and pearly white skin. Mermaids also speak the language of the coastline near where they appear and are known for their beautiful singing. Seals and manatees do not speak or sing.

The mer-folk—mermaids, in particular—have powers far beyond human capability. This fact about mermaids goes back as far as there is verbal or written history about these water creatures. They have been known to grant humans wishes and gifts, such as healing.

The mer-folk are more widely spread than most people realize. They exist in all kinds of water, an element that is not friendly to human habitation. Although most of the remaining legends concern the world's oceans and human-sized mermaids, smaller mer-folk and related water creatures inhabit every type of water on the face of this planet. Some mermaids exist only in lakes, reminding us of the Lady of the Lake that gave King Arthur the sword Excalibur. Others inhabit rivers, waterfalls, tiny streams, and even the wetland areas where water is almost under the surface of the earth instead of on top of it. The mer-folk are not the Elemental undines associated with the Element of Water. Rather, the mer-folk are a separate species, male and female, who work with the undines and have a distinct life and powers of their own.

The mer-folk are also adept at shapeshifting. If they do not wish to be seen, they can blend in with the surrounding environment so well that they become invisible to humans. The mer-folk can also remove their fishlike tails and walk on dry ground with two legs. There are only two ways to tell if an unknown person is a member of the mer-folk community.

First, they will not go far from whatever water they inhabit. They will have slight webs between their fingers and toes, and their skin will have a pearly sheen to it.

Mermaids are far less aggressive than mermen, the males of this species. This trait may be based on negative past experiences with humans. However, both male and female mer-folk have been known to interbreed on rare occasions with humans. Eventually, though, the mer-folk always return to their water home, leaving behind their human lover, and frequently the children born of that union. Certain human clans and families of Ireland, Scotland, and Wales claim descent from a human and mer-folk union; these families are marked with distinct webs of skin between their toes and often their fingers, too.

Among the powers of the mer-folk is their ability to affect the weather, particularly calling up or calming storms. Some stories tell of these creatures raising storms as retribution for a human breach of behavior or in self-defense. Other tales remark on their powers to calm storms so that friendly fishermen or mariners can make it safely to port. Because the Element of Water is closely connected with human emotions, the mer-folk also have the ability to affect human emotions. This can be a positive or negative trait, depending upon the behavior of the human in question and the goals of the mermaid or merman involved. Because they do have this power, they can teach humans how to change negative behavior patterns or life events into positive paths.

The mer-folk and many of the water creatures are great healers and forecasters of the future. Little is known of these traits, probably because humans have never taken the time or made the effort to befriend and learn from these amazing beings. It is time to reopen this ancient door to learning the secret powers of magick from the mer-folk. If one can learn to predict possible future paths, then we can make better choices in our lives. And no method of healing and magick should be discarded simply because we haven't heard of it before.

The universe holds so many mysteries of secret powers that we cannot hope to learn them all in a hundred lifetimes. Besides, an open, inquiring mind has been proven to add to human quality of life far into the older years. When one stops learning, one begins to age mentally.

Although the mer-folk have many human characteristics, they definitely are not human in their behavior and thinking, and we should not expect them to be like us. Being human does not make us better than other species, whatever plane of existence they inhabit.

With our present human concerns of preserving the Earth, as well as bettering our everyday life, we need to seek out the friendship and teaching of the mer-folk and other water creatures. Their concerns for preservation of the planet match ours, while their knowledge and powers exceed those of humans. The more we learn from the mer-folk, the stronger the bond

Secret Powers of the Mermaids

we can create between the two species. The stronger the bond, the more power we can use to improve life on all levels for both species. The more you learn as a person, the stronger and more self-confident you become. Add to this the cultivation of an unusual and powerful friendship with a species that has been on Earth as long as, if not longer than, humans, and the future opens up into a limitless series of opportunities.

So I welcome you to the world of magickal mermaids and other water creatures. May you learn amazing things that add to your life on all levels.

# CHAPTER 2

# Mer-Folk Legends

Almost all creation legends from around the world begin with an abyss of salt water and fresh water or earth that becomes mixed with the ocean. This mixture begins to create all things. Sometimes the universe is already in place, while other times this mating of Elements brings forth everything, including the universe. However, it is not the salt water itself that produces and creates. Rather, there is a female sea creature of great power that instigates the mating and thus the creation of all things. This female sea creature or goddess is the first version of a mermaid. There are stories of mermaids all around the world. Most of them describe the mer-folk as having scaled tails, but also as being able to put these aside and walk on the land. A few stories speak of the mermaids as having legs and looking much like humans. But the tails are always there in one form or another.

The following mermaid tales are samples of the worldwide variety of mer-folk stories. In fact, you would probably not expect mermaid stories from some of the countries listed.

## Babylonia

In early Babylonian legends, from the first millennium B.C.E., there is a sea creature called Tiamut. Carved images portray her as part winged animal and part shining serpent, similar to the iridescent tail of the traditional mermaid. When she deliberately mingled her salt water with the fresh water of Apsu, her consort, they created all the gods. This included Marduk, a solar god who dispelled Tiamat's darkness and then used her body to finish creating the Earth in all its diversity.

However, not all mermaids around the world are portrayed as half fish, half human. Many of them appear to be totally human, as those who leave behind their tails and come ashore to mingle with humans. But there is no doubt that these women are mermaids, for they live in the sea or a lake. Although often difficult to find, these wonderful tales still exist in the cultural history of many countries.

## Shetland Islands

Humans often try to hold a mermaid captive, as in the following story. However, it only proves satisfactory if the mermaid desires to stay with the human.

This story also shows that there is more than one type of oceanic mermaid, for the sea people here wear sealskins instead of fish tails. This makes them selkies, who are a branch or another cultural group of mer-folk.

One night, as a man walked along the beach of one of the Shetland Islands, he saw a large group of mermaids and mermen dancing in the light of the full moon. The sealskins that they wore while in the water were piled to one side. Transfixed, the man watched until the dance broke up, and the mer-folk donned their magickal skins. One by one, they leaped back into the water and disappeared.

Seeing one sealskin left on the beach, the man quickly grabbed it and ran home. To have a sealskin from a selkie was very lucky indeed. When the mermaid or merman came to retrieve it, the man could ask for a wish to be granted.

The next morning, curious as to why no mermaid had arrived to claim the skin, the man walked back down to the beach. There, he saw a beautiful woman sitting on a rock, tears running down her face. She told him she had lost her magickal skin and so could not return to her underwater home. At the sound of her voice, the man fell madly in love with her. He forgot about the wish in return for the skin. Instead, he asked the selkie to marry him; he would love her so much she would never miss her undersea home. Knowing she couldn't change his mind, the selkie agreed.

The two were married immediately. Before too long, the selkie wife bore the man two children. The man was very happy with his life, but the selkie constantly longed for the other selkies, her undersea life, and the freedom she had in the water. She would sit and gaze sadly at the ocean waves as they broke on the beach.

One day her little son discovered the sealskin his father had hidden. The boy carried it to his mother at the beach to share his new "treasure." The selkie was overjoyed to have her sealskin once more. She hugged and kissed her children for the last time, then slipped into her magickal skin and dove into the water. The man saw her as she went into the water but was too late to stop her. His selkie wife never returned.

This tale shows that mermaids are not reliable. Whether captured or living on land by choice, they all eventually return to their natural habitat. Their emotional attachment is not the same as that of humans to one another. However, this tale is different from others in that there was no retaliation by the

other selkies. Usually, when a mermaid of any kind was captured, their kin and friends created heavy mists, storms, gales, and shipwrecks. They cut off all trade and livelihood to the responsible human village. This was more than enough for the villagers to pressure the kidnapper into releasing his reluctant captive.

# Ireland

The Irish mermaid Liban is called the "Sanctified Mermaid." The Christians sanctioned her and carved her image in their churches. Said to be the daughter of Eochaid and Etain, her story began in the year 90 C.E.

Liban and her family lived near a sacred well that had been neglected for some time and was clogged so badly that the water no longer flowed out. One day the water of this well burst forth in such a huge amount that it formed the large lake Lough Neagh. The flood also drowned Eochaid and his family, except Liban, two of her brothers, and her pet dog, although the two brothers are never mentioned again.

As Liban struggled in the rolling floodwaters, she prayed that she and her dog would be saved. The girl was suddenly changed from the hips down into a salmon, while her upper body remained human. Her pet dog was turned into an otter. They finally made their way to the ocean, but Liban never strayed far from the shore.

Some of the local fishermen caught her in their nets and went to the Christian priest in a church nearby. The priest went down to the coast and decided, from her mermaid form, that Liban had no soul. He asked Liban if she wanted to gain a soul through Christian baptism or die right then. Liban chose the baptism, but died immediately afterward.

Liban's spirit can aid a student to learn how to accept harsh life changes.

# France

The following story tells about Melusine, one of the most famous European mermaids. Her form reminds one of the alchemical mermaid in the study of alchemy. She was human from the waist up but had a double fish tail as her lower body. She could appear as completely human for six days, but on the seventh day, she needed to assume her mermaid form and be in water.

A French count and his eldest son were on a boar hunt so long that they stopped and built a fire to warm themselves. As they sat by the fire, a boar charged at them. The son attacked with his sword, which bounced off the boar and killed his father instead. Afraid he would be accused of murder in order to inherit, the son rode his horse away from the scene. Soon he came to a moonlit glade in the forest where he found a bubbling fountain and three beautiful women wearing white dresses.

One of the women stepped forward to talk with him. When he asked where she came from, the woman put her finger on his lips and said, "Do not ask this so I will not have to lie to you. My name is Melusine. Come and talk with me."

The young man was so enchanted by Melusine that he told her of the accident and asked her advice. She bade him return to the castle alone, as all the other hunters would, and everyone would think the boar had killed the count.

The woman was so wise and charming that the young man sat talking with her until sunrise. Then he asked her to marry him. Melusine agreed, but only on two conditions: that he build her a castle at the fountain and that she be allowed to spend every Saturday at her castle with no one disturbing her. And if he invaded her privacy on Saturdays, she would leave him.

The young man returned to the castle, and no one suspected him of the accident that killed his father. As soon as the young man became the count and received his inheritance, he married Melusine in a splendid ceremony.

Melusine called her castle Lusignan. The villagers, who greatly loved and admired her, called her the Lady of Lusignan. Over the years, Melusine gave birth to many children, all of whom had some monstrous part to them. The first son had one red and one green eye. The second son had one eye higher in his head than the other. Another son had one boar's tusk protruding from his mouth.

Regardless of their deformities, the sons grew up to be outstanding men. Some became priests, while others became warriors. Although the count could never decide why the children were so hideous, he was very proud of their accomplishments and very much in love with their mother, Melusine.

One of the count's jealous younger brothers began to repeat all the gossip and speculation about Melusine's Saturday activities, hinting that she was entertaining men at the castle or holding meetings for witches. Although the count sent his brother away, he began to think about the strange agreement he had made years ago with his wife. By the next Saturday he was burning with suspicions.

He followed his wife through the woods to the castle Lusignan. Strangely, there were no noises inside. As the count quietly made his way through all the rooms of the castle, he heard nothing and saw no one. Finally, he came to the door of Melusine's dressing room and found the door locked. Peering through the keyhole, he was astonished to see that his wife's body, from the waist down, had changed into the big, blue tail of a fish.

The count crept out of the castle and raced through the woods home. He vowed never to tell anyone, not even Melusine, that he knew her terrible secret. Years passed while the count kept the secret. One day, however, horrible news reached him about one of his sons. The young man had attacked a nearby monastery, killing more than 100 monks, one of whom was his own brother.

The count went into a melancholy mood. He wondered if this was in retribution for accidentally killing his father years ago. Then he thought of Melusine's dark secret and decided that was the reason one of his sons would kill another. When Melusine tried to comfort him, he accused her of being a hateful serpent. Knowing her secret was out, she fainted.

When the count revived her, she wept and rushed out of the house. She left her footprint on the last stone she touched before plunging into the ocean. Melusine never returned, however, she kept track of her family.

Guy de Lusignan, one of Melusine's descendants, was the King of Jerusalem and Cyprus during the 12th century. The Lusignan family continued to rule in those two countries for more than three centuries. Before the death of any Lusignan family member, the mermaid appeared on the castle ramparts and piercingly cried like an Irish banshee. When her family line died out, she began to give death-warnings to the French kings.

The Lusignan family and Melusine were so famous that several other families, including those of Luxembourg and Rohan, changed their ancestry to include the mermaid in their pedigree.

Melusine can help you learn to manage money and learn how to use that money to make more. She can also make a student sensitive to disasters and approaching deaths.

## North America

A long time ago, according to a northern Native American tale, there lived a little girl whose name was Menana. She decided she wanted to walk among the stars in the heavens, so she begged the Great Spirit. She agreed to give up her physical body in order to do this. However, she soon became bored and asked to be returned to a human body. The Great Spirit warned her that this change would not be easy, but Menana kept begging until the Great Spirit agreed. However, Menana could not return to her former home; she would have to live with the spirits of the flood, who would adopt her as their daughter.

So Menana returned to live under a great waterfall with the spirits of the flood. At first, her physical body was that of a fish. Then, very slowly, it began to change into that of a girl again. When she became more human than fish, the Great

Spirit told her she could now live once more among humans. The change from fish into human would continue, but would never be completed until she fell in love.

When the ancient head warrior of the Ottawa nation stepped outside one morning to greet the rising sun, he was surprised to find a strange little creature there, half girl and half fish. Instead of legs, she had a fish tail, and her arms were covered with shining fish scales. When he asked her name, she answered, "Menana of the Waterfall." Accepting her as a gift from the Great Spirit, the warrior took her into his house as a daughter.

The Ottawa people loved her, for she told fantastic stories, sang like a bird, and plaited wonderful robes with mulberry bark and the feathers of war eagles. As she continued to live among the Ottawa, the fish scales fell from her arms and hands, and her tail turned into two human legs. However, her spirit was still as untamed as a sea creature. She dearly loved to swim in rushing rivers, dance in spring rains, and return to the waterfall to commune with the flood spirits.

One day, as she returned to the Ottawa camp from talking with the flood spirits, Menana found a group of Adirondack warriors smoking the peace pipe with her adopted father. Immediately, she saw a handsome young warrior chief named Piskaret. Unfraid, she walked straight up to Piskaret and asked, "How can I win your love?"

Piskaret immediately fell in love with her. "I already love you," he whispered in her ear. "Come and marry me now."

But the group of Adirondacks refused to let them marry, because they had heard of Menana and knew she came from the flood spirits. "The flood spirits have drowned our warriors and ruined our crops," they said. "You cannot marry."

The Adirondacks drove Menana away from her love, tied Piskaret up, and took him away with them.

Menana spent more and more time by the waterfall, singing sad songs and listening to the soothing voices of the flood spirits. One day Menana rushed back to her village and told everyone she was going back, to be one of the water spirits. Everyone tried to talk her out of the decision, but she would not change her mind. So the Ottawa nation solemnly followed her back to the waterfall. She waved to her friends and disappeared forever.

Later that afternoon, an Adirondack war party came down the river above the falls. It was led by Piskaret. Suddenly, the water spirits took on the appearance of warriors and waved their spears at the Adirondacks. Menana stood in the middle of the water spirits. When the ghost warriors started killing the Adirondacks, Menana protected Piskaret from the spears, throwing her arms around him, and the two sank together beneath the water. She turned Piskaret into a water spirit and married him beneath the waterfall.

## Japan

In the beginning of ancient Japanese history, an earthquake created a small green island with the World-Under-the-Sea surrounding it. This world was ruled by the Sea King and Queen. Their palace was made of shells, coral, marble, and precious gems.

The Sea King presided over the tides, rains, and floods. His breath created the wind that beat the waves into foam. He never left the sea, but the Queen often visited the little island, riding on the back of a mighty green dragon. When she set foot on land, she disguised herself as a court lady.

The Sea Queen loved the island so much that she built a summer palace there, planting vast beautiful gardens, mulberry plantations, and grain fields. She had many servants to care for her holdings when she returned for visits to the sea. However, it was not long before a terrible monster attacked her palace and land.

This malevolent serpent was called Ja. His mustache was made of snakes, his eyes blazed fire, he walked on a million legs, and he could coil seven times around Mt. Mikami. When the serpent visited the small island with the Sea Queen's palace, Ja ate all the fruit, grain, and servants. Then he destroyed the palace.

When next the Sea Queen visited, she screamed in horror at the devastation. "Will no one kill the serpent Ja for me?" she wailed.

Toda the Archer, a young warrior, was passing by at that time and heard the wailing plea. He did not know the woman but promised he would kill Ja for her.

As he searched the island for the great serpent, he planned what to do. He knew he could kill it if he moistened the tip of his arrow with saliva. Human saliva was deadly poison to Ja.

Toda kept hunting the serpent, even though it was twilight and he could see little. As he started to cross a bridge, two flames shot into the air as Ja thrust his head out of the mist. Toda fired an arrow but forgot to moisten it with saliva. The

arrow bounced harmlessly off the serpent's head. Toda held his ground as he notched another arrow. He moistened the tip with his saliva, and fired again at Ja. The arrow hit Ja directly in the forehead.

Ja roared in his anguish; the snakes in his mustache began to die. The serpent's long body jerked and finally stiffened as it died.

The Sea Queen came riding out of the night on her green dragon. Toda shielded his eyes from her brightness and asked who she was.

"I am the Sea Queen. Without knowing my name, you bravely consented to kill the serpent Ja, and did so. Now I wish to reward you."

The Sea Queen clapped her hands, and a boat made of shells rose to the surface of the sea. Toda climbed into the boat and was amazed as the boat followed the green dragon into the deep where the World-Under-the-Sea lay, with its glittering palace. Hundreds of sea fairies wearing robes of shells fringed with mother-of-pearl ran around Toda's boat. Following the Sea Queen's orders, the sea fairies filled Toda's boat with huge casks of rice, jars of wine, silk robes, a mighty sword, and a huge bronze bell. Then the fairies escorted the boat back up to the island's shoreline.

Toda's frantic servants came running, for they had searched everywhere for him. But when Toda tried to explain, he saw that the boat was gone and his gifts were lying on the sand. Later, the warrior discovered magickal qualities to all his gifts from the Sea Queen. The casks of rice and jars of wine never went empty. The silk robes did not wear out, and the mighty sword conquered all whom it touched.

After the time of Toda, the huge bronze bell was hung in a temple by a lake, where even today its sound wakes the monks and white herons each morning.

## China

In ancient China, a general was fishing on Tung Lake. When he saw a huge fish just under the surface, he shot it with an arrow and had it hung from the mast of the ship. However, a young man named Chen Pichiao was bothered by this and begged the general to release the fish. Finally, the general agreed. Chen put a piece of plaster over the wound and returned the fish to the lake.

A year later, Chen's small boat was caught in a sudden storm as he crossed Tung Lake. The boat sank, leaving Chen to float ashore on a bamboo crate. While resting beneath a willow, he heard the sound of galloping horses. He quickly hid behind a tree as a beautiful princess and her attendants rode by, carrying bows and arrows.

Chen hurried away from the lake, traveling over green hills, until he suddenly came upon a palace with high walls. Curious, he crossed a stone bridge, opened the red doors, and entered into a courtyard. There were swaying willows and tall elms filled with singing birds. The fragrance of flowers was everywhere. Even a swing hung from a cloud. When he heard horses galloping into the courtyard, Chen hid to watch the princess and her attendants play in the garden. As they wandered away, he followed, only to be captured by guards and thrown into prison.

When Chen was finally taken before the princess, she was astonished. "Forgive us," she said to him, "and please accept my gratitude."

Chen could not reason why this was happening, until the princess explained that she had been the fish the general shot with an arrow—the same one Chen had patched and released.

They had a great feast, and as Chen Pichiao danced with the princess, he realized he cared deeply for her. But after three days, he began to worry about his friends and family. The princess assured him that he could return to his family but that she would make it possible for him to visit her, too.

The next day, everyone in the village was surprised to see Chen ride up on a fine horse and wearing splendid clothes. With him he brought many valuable jewels with which he built a magnificent home. When he told everyone about what had happened to him, no one believed him.

Later, Liang, a friend of Chen's, was going across Tung Lake when he saw a beautiful barge and heard singing and music from it. When he peered inside, he saw Chen sitting with the lake princess. For several hours, Liang visited with them before returning to the village. But the first person he saw was Chen.

"How did you get here first?" Liang asked.

"I've been here all day," Chen answered, and his friends agreed.

"He can't be in two places at one time," Liang shouted. But everyone laughed at him.

After a very long and happy life, Chen died. As the men carried his coffin to the grave, they realized it was far too light. When they opened it, there was only a little seaweed and some water. The princess had done her final magick for Chen.

## Nigeria

A very beautiful girl from an African village turned down all offers of marriage, saying she would only marry the most handsome man in the land. While visiting the market one day, she spied a very handsome man and asked him to marry her.

He told her he would love to have her for a wife, but he could not, because he was not really a man. The gods had given him magickal power to appear as a man when he visited the land, but his real home as a fish-man was in the river at Idunmaibo.

The girl insisted that she would still marry him if he would promise to visit land from time to time. So they went to a certain place on the river, where they were married. Then the fish-man taught his wife a magick song that she was to sing there, along the river, so he would come to her.

Every day the girl made sweetmeats for her husband and took them to Indunmaibo. She sang the magick song, and her fish-husband came to sit with her on the riverbank. He brought her gifts of coral and gems from the sea. They were very much in love.

Then, one day, the girl's family told her she must marry. They were puzzled when she said she was already married but would not tell them who her husband was. When she took the basket of food to the river that day, her brother turned himself into a fly and followed her. He flew home at once to tell his parents. Horrified, they sent the girl to live with her father's people, far away from the river.

As soon as the grieving girl was gone, her brother took her father to the river at Idunmaibo. There, he sang the magick song, and the fish-man came up onto the bank. The father immediately stabbed him to death with a long knife. As he died, the fish-man's body shriveled and disappeared.

The girl was allowed to return home at once. Immediately, she fixed the basket of food, went to the river, and sang the magick song. Her husband did not appear. When she heard someone sing the song behind her, she turned to find her brother.

"The fish-man won't come to you anymore," the brother said. "Our father killed him."

"Then I will join my husband's spirit," the girl cried, and she jumped into the river.

Instead of drowning, she sank into the deep water and changed into an *onijegi*, or mermaid. Even today, people living along the river at Idunmaibo say you can sometimes hear the mermaids singing.

## Ukraine

When Tremsin was a tiny baby, he was carried off by an eagle that raised him until he was 16. Then the eagle kicked him out of the nest and told him to find his own way in the world.

As Tremsin sat frightened and sad on the ground, a talking horse approached him. The horse had only one piece of advice: if he ever found a feather from the Burning Bright Bird, Tremsin should not pick it up. It wasn't long before he discovered such a feather. Without a thought, Tremsin picked it up and rode on. Because he was raised by eagles, he was not harmed by the feather.

When he came to the estate of a rich nobleman, he asked for work and was given a job in the stables. He brushed the nobleman's horses until they shone like burnished silver. This made the other stableboys jealous, and they plotted to get rid of Tremsin. They went to the nobleman and told him Tremsin bragged he could get the Burning Bright Bird for him. The stableboys were certain their lie would cause Tremsin great trouble.

The nobleman called Tremsin to him and ordered the young man to bring the rare bird or lose his head. Tremsin told his troubles to his horse, who told him how to capture the Burning Bright Bird. Tremsin stripped off his clothes, lay down in the tall grass, and grabbed the bird by her leg when she swooped down to peck out his eyes. He then gave the bird to the nobleman.

The other stableboys were even more jealous. Again, they went to the nobleman and said that Tremsin bragged he could capture the thrice-lovely Nastasia, a mermaid from the sea. Again, the nobleman ordered Tremsin to do this task or lose his head.

In a white tent by the shore, the young man put out beautiful scarves, trinkets, fruits, and wine, following the advice of his horse. The mermaid Nastasia soon came out of the water to enjoy the luxuries. Then she fell asleep in the tent. Tremsin took her at once to the nobleman, who allowed the lad to keep the mermaid.

But Nastasia was not to be won over easily. She, too, demanded that Tremsin perform certain tasks. First, he had to find her coral necklace under the sea. He did this by enlisting the aid of a crab. When he returned it to the mermaid, she gave him the hardest task of all to win her love: he must gather from the sea her herd of wild horses, led by a thrice-terrible mare.

Tremsin's talking horse told him to get 20 animal hides, a whip, and a bridle for this task. The young man fastened the animal hides onto his horse's back. Then he waited on the shore while his horse swam out to Nastasia's herd. When the terrible mare and the herd turned to chase him, Tremsin's horse swam for the shore. Each time the mare caught up with him, she would bite and pull an animal hide off the horse's back, ripping it to shreds. This went on for 70 leagues across the sea.

As his horse came to the shore on a large billowing wave, Tremsin waded out and cracked the whip on the mare's forehead. When she came to a stop, he bridled her and rode her out of the sea, with the herd following.

However, the mermaid set the young man one last task before she would love him. He had to milk the mare, putting boiling hot milk in one barrel, lukewarm milk in a second barrel, and icy cold milk in the third barrel. Then Nastasia ordered Tremsin to jump in and out of each barrel, which he did. The first barrel turned him into an aged man, the second into a little boy, and the third into a very handsome man. Then Nastasia did the same, with the same results.

Finally, Nastasia and Tremsin were married. For half the year, they and their horses live under the sea. The other half of the year, they live on the Ukrainian steppes.

# Iran

A king of Persia had one hundred wives, but none of them bore him any children. One day a merchant showed up with a remarkable slave girl. Her hair fell in seven heavy braids to her ankles, and her eyes were so bright they healed the sick. The king fell in love with her and paid the merchant 10,000 gold coins for the girl. However, the girl wouldn't talk or move, because her heart was broken. The king tried everything to please the slave girl but nothing worked until the king professed his love for her and declared that he soon would die of grief if she didn't speak.

At this, the girl told him her name was Princess Julnare and her land was Land-Under-the-Sea. She was a child of the sea who wandered ashore in the moonlight, only to be captured by a slave merchant. The king apologized for the ways of men.

"Because of your kindness," Julnare said, "I will give you a child."

The next year, a plump, rosy-cheeked boy was born to Princess Julnare. The king's joy knew no bounds. He ordered seven days of celebration, gave gifts to the poor, released all prisoners, and freed all his slaves.

At the naming ceremony on the eighth day, the Princess named her son Smile-of-the-Moon. Then she asked the king to let her send for her mother, Queen Locust of the Sea, and her brother, Prince of the Sea, so they could bless the child. When she put two pieces of sweet-smelling wood on the fire and whispered magickal words, the sea parted and two people walked on the surface of water, then leapt upward through the window, as light as foam. The handsome youth with rosy-cheeks and sea-green hair was Prince of the Sea. The old woman with white hair and a ruby crown was Queen Locust of the Sea.

They kissed Princess Julnare with tears of joy. The Princess put her son in her brother's arms. The Prince kissed the baby a thousand times, then leapt out of the window with him into the sea.

"My son! My son!" the king cried as he ran toward the window.

"Wait," Princess Julnare whispered to her husband, as she pointed at the waves below. The sea opened, and Prince of the Sea appeared with Smile-of-the-Moon still in his arms. When the Prince leapt back through the window, the king saw that the baby was sound asleep.

"Were you afraid when I jumped into the sea with the baby?" the Prince asked.

"Yes," the king admitted. "I thought he would drown and I would never see him again."

"I gave him the same birthright as all the children of the sea," the Prince said. "He will never drown."

Princess Julnare's mother and brother leapt through the window, back into the sea. The Sea Princess of Persia lived happily with her king from then on.

# CHAPTER 3

# Seeking Water Folk for Friendship and Help

As long as there have been written records or memorized stories, there have been indications that the mer-folk inhabited the waters of this planet. There is speculation that the mer-folk were created on Atlantis during genetic experiments, and that the collapse and destruction of that civilization released them into the ocean. Others believe the mer-folk have always been astral/Earth creatures, like the faeries, and that they are able to move back and forth between the astral plane and Earth at will. However this species originated, most of these beings are friendly toward humans.

Because this planet is primarily composed of water, and water is a vital and necessary ingredient of human life—in fact, to all life—learning to work with the mer-folk should be important to us. Not only do we need to know the Earthly powers inherent in the Element of Water, but we also need to relearn the ancient magick behind Water itself. The only way we can relearn this magick is from the mer-folk, masters of the Element of Water. And they will not teach us until we gain their friendship and trust. Thus, we vitally need to draw the mer-folk into our lives. Humans need to regain all the ancient, lost knowledge that we can.

Cultivating a friendship with all species of mer-folk can also be of help to us when we face disasters or merely problems that involve water (either physical water or the Element of Water). This water species can teach us to control our emotions, too. With our physical bodies being mostly liquid, we frequently experience difficulties with our emotions.

To begin a friendship with the mer-folk, you can record the following meditation into a tape recorder and replay it when you meditate. During this meditation, allow yourself to experience as many of the qualities of water as you can, knowing that you are perfectly safe underwater and are in no danger of drowning. Meditation allows you to safely enter areas and objects without any physical harm whatsoever.

## Meeting the Mer-Folk

Sit in a comfortable chair with your hands in your lap and your feet flat on the floor. Make certain you will not be disturbed by the telephone, someone at the door, pets, or any other people in the house.

Visualize a brilliant white light surrounding and penetrating your body. This is your protection throughout the meditation. Now, slowly begin to relax your body, beginning at the feet and ending at the head.

Now you are standing on a small knoll of sand, with a long beach on one side of you and a series of low rock formations on the other. The sun has dropped behind the horizon, leaving a beautiful sunset blazing across the sky. The bright, glowing colors are reflected in the ocean waves from far out right onto the shoreline. There is a hint of coolness in the small breeze coming in from the ocean.

You turn toward the rocky side of the shore and begin to make your way across the rocks. From time to time, you stop and admire the tiny crabs and other sea animals in the tidal pools among the rocks. Finally, you come to a rock that has a series of flat ledges on its side. These ledges lead up to a wider flat platform that gives you a perfect view of the ocean and the sunset. Steps also lead down the other side of the rock to a large, flat stone that is barely covered with water as the waves slide over it.

As you stand, watching the waves bring in the light of the setting sun, you begin to think about mermaids and mermen. How wondrous and amazing it would be to see and talk with one of the mer-folk, you think. There are surviving stories of such encounters, so why could it not happen to you?

Your attention is caught by two ripples coming in across the waves to the flat stone near you. Suddenly, what looks like a large fish tail flashes above the water, then smacks the waves as if to draw your attention. You start down the other steps that lead to the large flat stone, carefully watching the ocean as you descend. The tail scales had been an unusual iridescent color, not at all like you would see on a shark or other large fish. You are curious about what the creature might be, and why it should want to attract your attention with the slap of its tail on the water.

As you reach the step above the flat rock, two heads pop up out of the water. The hands grasping the rock have webs between the fingers. The facial features are very humanlike, the skin extremely pale, and the hair long and white with a slight green tint to it. The being with shorter hair is wearing a red cap. You recognize him as a male. As the other being pulls herself onto the flat rock, you see that her breasts are covered with a net of colorful seashells and tied with seaweed strands. From her waist down she has brilliant scales on her lower portion and tail. You realize that they are mer-folk, the answer to your quest.

"Come," calls the merman, as he beckons with one hand. "We will show you the wonders of the ocean."

"Yes," the mermaid agrees, "you must learn all about water in order to work with us." She smiles as she takes your hand, "You will be in no danger with us, and can breathe underwater without any trouble."

You step hesitantly down onto the water-covered, flat rock, looking at the waves coming in and splashing on the rocks. The merman takes your other hand. Suddenly, they both jerk you into the water with them.

After a brief moment of surprise and fear, you realize that you can breathe underwater with no problem. As the mer-folk pull you along, into the deeper parts of the ocean, you watch schools of fish swim by, crabs and other creatures on the sandy floor below you, and an octopus swiftly slip away.

Then you hear the merman's voice inside your mind: "Just think your questions, and we will hear you."

"Open your inner mind," the mermaid urges. "Feel the different textures of the water around you. The swirling currents make each area of water feel slightly different. Some swirls are warmer than others. Some rougher, some smoother."

As the mer-folk continue to pull you along, you close your eyes and try to feel with your skin. Soon, you can detect the differences in water temperature and change in the feel of water against your body. All at once, you feel stronger eddies of currents coming from something large ahead of you. You open your eyes to see the first of several mer-folk cities.

This city appears to be enclosed in a bubble, yet the water easily comes and goes through this nearly invisible barrier, as do the mer-folk moving about the area.

"The dome is a safety wall to protect us from aggressive ocean creatures and other negative water beings," the merman explains. "The magick built into it can detect negativity and forbid entry to whatever or whoever is guilty of this emotion. In this manner, we may safely raise our children, live, and work."

You feel a slight pull against your skin as the mer-folk take you through the protective bubble into the city. You look around to see colorful houses made of living coral and sea rocks, with gardens of sea anemones and other stationary ocean plants. In the center of the city are quite large buildings that are more elaborately decorated than the others.

The mer-folk take you straight to the central building of the colorful compound. At the door, they explain their mission to the guard, who signals them on. Before long, you find yourself in a large room dominated by two tall chairs on a plat-form. Other mer-folk are gathered in groups about the room, talking and eating small pieces of food that look like pastries. The mer-folk accompanying you take you straight to the tall thrones, where a merman and mermaid sit, each wearing a small crown.

"This human is ready to learn more about the mer-folk, water itself, and its connection with all the Elements," your merman says with a bow.

The king and queen smile as they beckon you to come for-ward. They spend time talking to you before they summon a mermaid wearing a dazzling stone in a necklace. She is a spe-cial teacher who will now help you to work on your necessary connections with the mer-folk and the Element of Water.

You go with her out of the palace to what appears to be a sea-garden. The two of you sit on a rock bench as she begins to teach you the first things you need to know about mer-folk: there is more than one group or culture of them, and not all mer-folk are alike.

After a time, your mer-folk come and return you to the flat rock at the edge of the shore where you started your journey. You find you are not wet, neither do you have any breathing problems. As you start to climb the rock stairs to the upper plat-form, you swirl away into a brilliant cloud and back into your physical body. You take three deep breaths, open your eyes, and the meditation is ended. (See Chapter 14 for additional meditation information.)

If you are near the ocean, a river, or small stream, you can attract the attention of local mermaids by arranging patterns of the local stones and fallen twigs. At the coast, you can use seashells in these patterns. Make the first pattern a small circle, which represents that all are of one energy. The second pattern is a five-pointed star that symbolizes the similarities between humans and the mer-folk. The third pattern, a plus mark, goes between the other patterns. The entire set of symbols is a form of language that says: *We are all one in the universe and should work together for benefits of both sets of beings.*

The local mermaids will find this message, and will be able to tell by your scent and vibrations on the stones and twigs if you are serious and exactly who you are. They can make themselves known to you through thoughts and dreams, the rearranging of the message symbols, or showing themselves in a very brief personal appearance.

Mermaids are helpful in learning to forecast the weather, and they sometimes make small changes in it. They do this by working with the air currents and the temperature of water currents nearby. In order to learn to do this, you must sit quietly outdoors with your eyes closed. Let your body become very aware of the air moving around you. Notice the changes in direction of the wind, or movement of air without wind.

When you have become very sensitive to the air whenever you go outside, it is time to meditate near water. Never sit too close to the shoreline at the beach because of the changing tides. Stretch your mind out and feel the differences in parts of water—how the water near shore feels and moves in different ways than the deeper water farther out. The same applies to rivers and streams. In a small stream, for example, the water at the center will be greatly different from that along the edges, because the mass is more astrally compact in a smaller area.

When you have gotten the feel of air and water, the next step is to meditate on maneuvering clouds and high wind currents to turn away storms or bring in rain.

The first project is to build your confidence in your ability to affect clouds. It is a game you may have played as a child. Lie down outside and look at the sky. Choose a small cloud to begin practice. Stare at the cloud as if your eyes are a laser beam that can cut a hole through it. Concentrate very hard on making that hole or splitting the cloud into two parts. You should be able to see a little progress in about 15 minutes on the first try. The cloud will either develop a noticeable hole in it or split into two parts that drift away from each other. After that first time, cloud-splitting may not take you as long.

As water evaporates from the oceans, it condenses into small particles of water and forms clouds. Depending upon the temperature of the surrounding air, these clouds release their water load in the form of rain, hail, or snow.

Each type of cloud signals a different kind of weather. Cirrus clouds are high in the troposphere, where the winds make them look thin and wispy. They are usually associated with pleasant weather. Stratus clouds, formed in the lower troposphere, cover most of the sky with an even, gray color similar to a fog. Stratus, some cumulus, and nimbostratus produce light rains. Cumulonimbus clouds are very tall, dense clouds that can be shaped like an anvil or block. They can correspond to tornadoes, hurricanes, thunderstorms, hail, lightning, and other violent forms of weather.

Understanding and working with clouds is only the first part of weather-working learned from the mer-folk. Practice applying a light force of mental will against the side of a cloud to make it move marginally off its course. Pushing at the front edge would be like butting heads with a bull, while applying pressure to the side of the cloud near the front will accomplish more success. Done properly, weather-working can be very tiresome, as a tremendous amount of energy is expended.

When working with air currents and storms, you need to call upon the local mer-folk for aid. You will be dealing with much more powerful elements than clouds. And until you are more expert in knowing where and when to apply pressure, you will need the help of the mer-folk to avoid mistakes and the possibility of making the weather worse than it is.

Sit in a meditative position indoors or outside. Start by mentally inviting the local mer-folk to join you and teach you how to make the weather better for your particular area. When you feel the breezy presence of the mer-folk, listen carefully to the flow of thoughts that goes through your mind. You will recognize their thoughts because they will not be in the words you might use or in the opinions you may have formed on the subject.

Because the mer-folk have been working the weather for centuries and centuries, they will know whether you should make any changes at all. Also, they know exactly how much pressure can be applied without creating a storm in another locality. When working the weather, you must be careful that you do not send powerful energy into another area's central

weather pattern in such a way that causes violent or dangerous storms. The Finnish magicians who worked closely with
the Elements and magickal powers were known and feared
throughout Europe and Russia for their ability to manipulate
the weather and cause great storms.

The first part of working the weather is to use your mind
to locate the different flows of air energy in the sky around you.
There will always be at least one major airstream, known as
the jet stream. This is the biggest and widest flow of air energy
anywhere around you and is the most difficult to influence.
Sometimes the jet stream will split in half, forming two strong
bands of energy. The jet stream is also the easiest to find with
your mind, and the most influential on the world's weather
patterns.

Other distinct flows of air you will quickly learn to recognize are high and low pressure systems. The high pressure systems run clockwise in their movement, while the low pressure
systems turn counterclockwise. These systems can range from
a mile or so wide to hundreds of miles in width. They have the
power to deflect the flow of the jet stream and, according to
the season of the year, herald a vast change in heat or cold. For
example, in the Pacific Northwest, the appearance of a high
pressure system in the summer can predict days of extremely
hot weather until the jet stream finally pushes it further east.
However, in the winter, that same high pressure system is a
harbinger of days of very cold weather.

The jet stream, the winds, and the high and low pressure
systems are invisible to human eyes. You can learn to find
these with your mind when helped and taught by one of the
mer-folk. Most people would object to linking the mer-folk

with the weather. However, if you consider the fact that in the United States on an average day there are forty trillion gallons of water in the sky above your head, you can immediately see the connection between the weather and mermaids.

Begin your explorations of the sky currents by asking for the help of a mermaid or merman who may live nearby. Entice her or him by having a blue or blue-green candle in a holder, sea salt, a small bowl of clean water, a spoon, a seashell, and a small vial of lotus oil. This ritual can be done at your personal altar or a flat, bare spot of earth outside. Visualize your working area as a circle just big enough to hold your magickal tools. Set the blue or blue-green candle in the holder at the top of the circle, in the north. Arrange the small bowl of water in the east and the little container of sea salt and the spoon in the west. Place the seashell and vial of lotus oil before you in the southern area of the small circle.

Every article in your ritual area represents an aspect of the sea, which is so closely connected with the mer-folk. Even the lotus oil is distilled from a flower that grows in water, its beautiful blossoms floating on the surface of pools and ponds.

Light the candle and say:

*The color of the mighty seas surrounds me. In its color can be found all the other colors of water upon the Earth.*

Hold the small bowl of water in your left hand while you slowly dribble a tiny amount of sea salt into the water. As you stir the salt into the water, say:

*I stir the waters of time in search of one of the mer-folk to come to me as a teacher of ancient magick.*

Set the bowl with the spoon in it in the center of the ritual area and say:

*As I patiently wait for the salt to blend with the water, so do I wait for the mer-teacher who will work well with me.*

Remove the top of the vial of oil. With the forefinger of your right hand, dab three separate spots of lotus oil onto the shell. Replace the lid on the oil. Hold both hands over the shell while saying:

*Mermaid, merman, hear my plea. As I will, so shall it be.*

Sit quietly for at least five minutes, reaching out with your mind and emotions, thus creating a mental welcome to your new teacher. Sometimes, their presence is heralded by a brisk chill over your body, or a deep sense of calm that wraps around you. When your instincts tell you that your teacher has arrived, dip your forefinger into the bowl of salted water and touch the center of your forehead just above and between your eyes. This is the area of the mystical Third Eye. Say:

*Let my mind be open to learning the ancient knowledge of Water.*

Sit for another few minutes, in case your new teacher has something to tell you. This will be very unlikely the first time

or two. The mer-teacher will be busy making her- or himself familiar with your aura and mental patterns. You should do meditations to learn the same things about your new teacher.

In order to become friends with all the types of mer-folk, you must practice respect for water in all its forms and for the land and plants surrounding it. By respecting water, you are respecting the homes and environment of these magickal, mystical beings.

The mer-folk are capable of granting wishes and giving humans psychic powers. If you are self-disciplined, sincere, and dedicated to your studies of Water magick, they will enrich your life in many ways. However, if you are not, you will discover the opposite effects afflicting you.

The mer-folk can be strong protectors, especially of women and children. They can also teach you how to predict storms and future events, as well as leading you to treasures. From them you can learn the value of freedom, imagination, and wisdom.

# CHAPTER 4

# Mermaids and Other Magickal Creatures of the Oceans

It seems appropriate to discuss general knowledge and characteristics of the mer-folk species before going into greater detail of specific subspecies.

The mer-folk have been known all around the world, including landlocked areas, long before history was recorded. We can deduce from ancient tales that there are a wide variety of mer-folk, both in appearance and behavior in their interaction with humans. However, there are enough similar traits among these types to indicate that they all belong to the same major species. For example, the European mer-folk exhibit certain characteristics that connect them as distant relatives of the Nereids of the Mediterranean.

The terms *mer-folk, mermaid,* and *merman* can be traced back to the Indo-European root *mori-*or *mari-*, which means "sea."

This ancient root carried over into the German *meer*, "sea"; the Latin *mare*, "sea"; the English *mere*, "lake, sea"; and the French *mer*, "sea."

In the northern European areas, most of the recorded sightings have been along the coastlines of Ireland, Cornwall, Wales, Scotland, and the British Isles in general. They are even seen along the rugged cliffs and fjords of the Scandinavian countries. Here, in the colder waters of the Atlantic where the coasts are rugged, the mer-folk seem to be abundant. Whether this is because fewer humans frequent or inhabit these areas, we do not know. There are also more undersea caverns and crevices in these areas, so either conjecture is a logical explanation.

However, different species of the mer-folk have been seen near China, the South Seas, along both coasts of North and South America, Africa, and the Indonesian areas. If one were to closely study all the folktales of every country that touches the ocean, I suspect you would turn up mermaid tales for all of them.

In the ancient history of Babylon, there was a fish-god, whom the people believe taught humans the arts of civilization. From early Assyrian records into the Persian era, surviving paintings and engravings show priests of this god practicing their healing and exorcism magick. They are wearing very strange ceremonial outfits that consist of fish heads pulled over the tops of their heads, with their human faces showing, while the fish bodies hang down their backs.

Throughout the ancient Middle Eastern cultures of Assyria, Babylon, and Mesopotamia, archaeologists have discovered early images of the mer-folk. These images have the traditional upper body of a human and lower body of a fish. The Assyrians called these beings *kulullu* (fish-man) and *kuliltu* (fish-woman). Sculptures of the mer-folk were found not only in palaces and temples, but smaller statues were used in private homes as part of protective magick.

In the Polynesian culture, the father of both humans and the gods was called Vatea; he was said to be half-human and half-porpoise. Several Native American tribes have a legend telling of a fish-man with green hair who led their starving people to the North American continent.

To the Germans, the mermaid was the *lorelei*, the *meriminni*, or the *meerfrau*, while in Iceland these beings were called the *marmenill*. In Denmark they are called the *maremind*, while the French know them as the *morgans* or *morgens*. Thousands of miles away from Europe, the *matsyanaris* of India are pictured as nymphs with fish tails.

The most famous mermaid in Africa is Yemaya. Her hair is composed of long green strands of seaweed, while her jewelry is all made of seashells. Today, Yemaya is considered a goddess of African culture.

Although mermen are known and written about in old stories, Europeans usually think only in terms of mermaids. Perhaps this is because mermaids present a more enticing picture than a merman does. Both are human-looking down to the hips with a fish's tail with large flukes, but no dorsal fin. However, the mermaid, being the natural creature she is, rarely covers her bare breasts. Even with the tales told over and over through the centuries, human males have refused to believe the repeated behavioral characteristics of mermaids. The mermen are usually less dangerous or tricky than the mermaids.

Although the mer-folk do like to sit on rocks in bays and soundings, their lives are lived primarily underwater. No one has ever mentioned that they have gills, but records do state that they have webs between the fingers and the toes. Because the mer-folk can breathe in both water and air, their physical construction must include both lungs as humans have, and some sort of alternative water-breathing lung. They must also be capable of switching between these functions on an automatic basis, for the stories say nothing of the mer-folk ever having difficulties going from sea to land and back again.

Their human-looking bodies from the hips up have skin that shimmers like silver over a pearly white undercoat. Their hair is usually a silver blonde, strawberry blonde, or a light brown. There is always a slight greenish tint to their hair and fingernails. Their eyes can be any shade of green to blue-green. It is not unusual for them to decorate themselves with discarded seashells or bits and pieces of jewelry found in old wrecked ships.

Mermaids, in particular, are fond of combing their hair. These combs are made of thin shells. They also wear combs to hold their hair high on their heads. If they find a mirror, it is considered to be prized possession. They often wear strings of pearls and shells around their necks.

Although both mermaids and mermen are very beautiful and alluring, it is a cold kind of beauty. Their emotional behavior is totally different from that of humans. The mer-folk do have deep feelings for those of their kind, but it is rare for that expressive emotion to extend to the human species. Like the water that sustains them, their emotions are fluid and changeable. Their ethics are also different, as is their entire way of thinking, planning, and working magick.

Because the mer-folk develop slowly and are immortal, unless deliberately killed, it is not possible to tell the ages of any mer-folk with whom you may work. Old tales say these beings have no souls. They do have souls, but not in the way as humans understand the word *soul*. They consider themselves a living part of the Supreme Power, as is everything else in this sphere of existence, so they have souls as does everything else. Human storytellers call the mer-folk vain, very jealous, and unforgiving to any humans who offend them, which is a human view of any species or culture that is different.

However, humans who are fortunate enough to speak with a mermaid or merman will not hesitate to ask the being to foretell their future, or ask the mer-person to bestow supernatural powers upon them. The mer-folk are very powerful with Water magick, seeing into the future, healing, and weather control. If you are blessed with a mermaid or merman as a special teacher, you will be taught all general mer-folk magick, while specializing in one area, and your own natural, inborn psychic talents will be strengthened.

Some of the mer-folk prefer to live in isolated family groups or small communities, traditionally where there are secure, comfortable caves to use as housing. In the South Seas area and other warmer climes where great coral reefs grow, they would discreetly fashion small places for themselves within the reef itself. However, most of the mer-folk prefer to live in a city-type setting, originally in deeper waters where they would not be disturbed by humans. They build magnificent palaces, both large and small, which they decorate with gold and jewels, most of this salvaged from ancient shipwrecks. They do not collect this "treasure" for its monetary value, but rather for its decorative uses.

All mer-folk have their own language, with several different dialects, depending upon where the groups live. However, they also know and understand the language of the humans living along their section of coast. By knowing the human language, they can pass on information to other mer-folk or communicate with the local humans. They are also very adept at telepathy, which they prefer when communicating with their human students. Mermaids also use their magickal singing to communicate over distances, much as whales use a type of sonar or echolocation. Their singing is particularly powerful when used near or in large oceans.

The mer-folk live on special herds of fish that they care for and other seafood. They are very careful to only choose full-grown fish. They also harvest undersea vegetation as part of their meals. They rarely interfere with fishermen unless that human has offended them in some manner or is overfishing a certain area, thus putting the ecology in jeopardy. Although some tales tell of capturing a mermaid or merman in a fishing net, this is quite unlikely. The mer-folk are very strong, sea-wise, and agile. Only if they were injured or ill would they fall victim to human fishermen.

Mermaids like to sit on rocks just out of the water and sing, while combing out their long hair. Combing the hair while working magick is an old secret, one that evidently the Scottish women learned, for in certain fishing towns it was considered a crime for a girl or woman to comb her hair while the fishing fleet was out. The voices of mermaids are very bewitching and, in the past, have been the cause of many ships wrecked on rocks and against cliffs. An angry mermaid, though, is much more dangerous. She can call up fierce winds and howling storms as she dances across the top of the foamy waves.

Both mermaids and mermen have the ability to remove their fish tails, revealing humanlike legs. They roll up the skin and deposit it among the rocks. Then they can dance along the sandy beach or walk about on dry land and mingle with humans, unnoticed. It is possible that some of the mer-folk spend much of their time, in and out of the water, with legs instead of the scaled tail. This may be because there is a strong physical attraction between the mer-folk and humans. However, because of the vast difference in emotions and character, dalliances and unions between the two groups do not last.

During the times that the mer-folk allowed themselves to be seen more frequently, human males would spy on mermaids as they came out of the water, removed their tails, and danced under the light of the moon. Many of these males fell in love with a mermaid and used trickery to force her to marry him. The trickery usually was to hide the skin, a shell necklace, or some other valuable possession of the mermaid. Thus, she was forced to stay on dry land until she could retrieve the hidden object. Many of these mermaids had children who were human rather than mer-folk. But the mermaid was always unhappy, looking longingly at the ocean. At some point, either she or one of her children would find the hidden object that kept her bound to the land. She then returned immediately to the water without a single glance at the family she left behind.

However, in a few cases, it was the human husband who became disenchanted with his mermaid wife and her strange behavior. He would return her skin tail and send her back to the sea. A few of these mermaids pined away and died on the nearby rocks on the shore. Sometimes, though, the rejected mermaid sought revenge, as in a tale of the Native American Adirondack tribe. One of the Adirondack men got tired of his mermaid wife and banished her from his village. The mermaid went back to the sea, only to return with other powerful mer-folk and water beings. They used their Water magick to call up a giant tidal wave that drowned the husband and flooded out the entire village.

In a few ancient stories, humans held the temporarily discarded skin of one of the mer-folk so they could force the mermaid or merman to reveal some secret knowledge or grant them a supernatural power, such as healing or foretelling. The humans would find out later that forcing the mer-folk to grant them their wish came with a problem: the knowledge or power always had one flaw in it.

The mermaids always lived with human males on land during their brief, passionate relationships. When mermen fell in love with a human woman, they turned their lover into an amphibious form and took them into the deep oceans to live in the fantastic cities there. Very few of these women ever chose to return to land.

The offspring of a mer-person and a human always had small webs between their fingers and/or toes. They were human in appearance and could not breathe underwater, although they were excellent swimmers. Some of these children also inherited predictive powers from their mer-folk parent.

During the medieval times, when the study of alchemy flourished and ceremonial magick was practiced, the alchemists turned the *siren* (previously known as a bird-woman) into a double-tailed mermaid. Ancient surviving books of alchemy call this kind of siren the "Siren of the Philosophers," or "Fish-Tailed Aphrodite Marina." She is always portrayed as holding the end of one of her fish tails in each hand, thus creating an obvious sexual symbol. The alchemists may have considered the siren as a mixture of mermaid and the Irish sexual Sheila-Na-Gig.

The mer-folk in general can grant wishes to human students or give some of them psychic powers. However, you must

be self-disciplined and dedicated in the study of Water magick for your life to become enriched.

Although there is an overall, general species known as the mer-folk, there are subspecies who have developed either slightly different looks or behavior patterns, as demonstrated in old tales and traditional accounts.

## Ben-Varrey

People on the Isle of Man call the mermaids who frequent their shores by the name of Ben-Varrey. Like other mermaids, these beings can enchant humans or lure them to their death in the sea by singing. However, the Ben-Varrey have a much softer side as shown by three old tales.

A fisherman once discovered a stranded Ben-Varrey and carried her back to the sea. As a reward, he was told where he could find a treasure. In a second story, a baby mermaid coveted a little human girl's doll so much that she stole it, while the child played on the sandy beach. The baby's mother scolded her child and made her return the doll along with a string of pearls. During one fishing season off Spanish Head, the fishermen of the nearby village were out fishing when a friendly Ben-Varrey rose out of the water. "Sail to land," she shouted. Those who trusted the mermaid immediately raced their boats to shelter in the bay. Those who did not believe in her were caught in a sudden strong storm, and lost all their tackle and, in some cases, their lives.

The Ben-Varrey mermaids can teach you how to handle emotions without bottling them up or letting them explode.

# The Blue Men

Fortunately, this particular subspecies is found only in Scotland, in the strait between Long Island and the Shiant Islands. They are most definitely not friendly toward humans and are known as the Blue Men of the Muir or the Minch. The females of the Blue Men stay in their underwater cave homes, while the males attack ships. They throw boulders and raise storms in the North Sea in an effort to wreck ships. The traditional way to stop their attack was for the ship's captain to speak to them in rhyme only while the ship continued on its way. Apparently, it took the Blue Men time to unravel the rhyming talk, which also allowed the sailors and their ship to escape.

There are several groups of the Blue Men living in this particular strait. Each group has its own underwater cavern and is ruled by a chieftain. Their group structure is very similar to the Scottish clans.

It is best to avoid trying to work with the Scottish Blue Men.

# The Ceasg

Even the Highlands of Scotland has a type of mermaid that lives in the cold sea along the Scottish shores. This mermaid is called the *ceasg* (pronounced *kee-ask*), or "Maiden of the Wave." She has the usual human female body down to the hips, but a large salmon tail. The ceasg is listed among the dangerous types of mer-folk. The only way to overcome her powers is to destroy her soul, which she keeps hidden somewhere. Sometimes the hiding spot is an egg, a shell, or a box. Highland fishermen were willing to take the chance of capturing a ceasg, for if they did, she had to grant them three wishes. If the fisherman could get the ceasg to live with him, his good fortune would become greater. Several famous Scottish pilots claimed ancestry of a ceasg and a human male.

Do not work with a *ceasg*, for you can never trust her information.

## Dinny-Mara

The Isle of Man has mermen called the Dinny-Mara or the Dooinney Marrey (pronounced *dunya mara*). These gentle, friendly mermen are good fathers. They like to romp in the waves with their children and bring them presents.

The Dinny-Mara can teach you to have more patience, be more family-oriented, and set time aside for family and fun.

## Cornish Mermaids

The mermaids along the shores of Cornwall are trickier and more sinister than most others, and their mermen less friendly, even to their own family. The mermen have been known to eat their own children. If caught by a fisherman, accounts tell us, the Cornish mermaid had to grant three wishes, but she usually managed to drown her captor before he could get back to shore. Avoid this dangerous mermaid for she only brings troubles with her.

# Hai Ho Shang

The Hai Ho Shang (sea Buddhist priest), or the sea bonze, is feared by fishermen who sail in the South China Sea. This creature has a shaved Buddhist monk's head but the body of a large fish. It is aggressive and very strong—so strong that it can seize and capture fishing boats and junks, pulling them under the water and drowning the entire crew.

There are only two ways to repel the Hai Ho Shang. One method is to burn feathers, but the second method is more effective. Someone has to perform a set ritual dance. At one time it was common for at least one sailor aboard each junk to be trained in this ritual dance, in addition to being responsible for his own duties.

The Hai Ho Shang is too dangerous to work with. It is best avoided.

# The Merrow

In Ireland the mer-folk are called the merrow. Although some people say that the murdhuacha (pronounced *mur-roo-cha*) are the same as the merrow, this is not true. The murdhuacha are sea cows.

Both sexes of the merrow are quite beautiful, although parts of their appearance can be startling. They all have fish tails, which they can remove to walk on land, and webbed fingers. The females have long, flowing green-tinted white hair and very dark green or blue eyes. Their upper bodies are covered with delicate, tiny, white scales that make them gleam in the moonlight or sunlight. The males are quite different in appearance. They have short arms that look like flippers and long red noses.

Their hair and teeth are green, and their eyes small. Both male and female merrows wear red caps. These caps aid them in traveling through the water. They cannot return to the sea if their caps are stolen or hidden. The merrow often fell in love with humans, married, and lived with them longer than others of the mer-folk. The children of these unions were usually covered with tiny scales all over their bodies. They also had small webs between the fingers and toes. This subspecies of mer-folk are very gentle, quite friendly to humans they meet, and happy with their lives. However, the Irish always dreaded it when the merrow appeared, for it meant that a storm was coming. The merrow are very adept at predicting storms, especially rain.

## The Nereids

There are fifty of these sea nymphs who live in the Mediterranean Sea. They are the granddaughters of Pontus, an old sea god, and Gaia, the Earth Mother. The Nereids do not have fish tails, although many of their other characteristics are similar to mermaids. Instead, they are beautifully formed women who wear short embroidered vests and harem-like pants. They are very vain, carefully braiding their long black hair and twisting it into an elaborate style atop their heads. They outline their dark eyes with a sea dye.

Most of their time is spent playing with and riding the dolphins, which are close allies with the mer-folk, especially the Nereids. They dart through the waves, following ships to distract the crew.

Whenever Amphitrite, the wife of Poseidon, takes out her sea chariot, the Nereids accompany her, riding on dolphins. Poseidon has the Tritons to surround his ocean chariot.

Although the Nereids are slightly irresponsible, they are very good at magickal spells concerning beauty, happiness, and balancing the emotions.

## The Nine Daughters of Ran

In Norse tales, Aegir, the god of the sea, was married to Ran, a death deity of the ocean. Ran used her nets to capture the souls of all those who perished in the sea, whether it was by drowning or through burning in a funeral boat. Although Aegir was a jovial god, who brewed ale and had great feasts for the other Norse deities, Ran and her nine daughters were not so amiable. They disliked humans and took every opportunity to cause misery and death. However, the daughters were quite beautiful, as are all mermaids.

These nine daughters were sea-giantesses, with names such as Bylgja ("wave"), Dufa ("diveress"), Hefring ("the lifting one"), Kolga ("wave"), Gjolp ("howler"), Greip ("grasper"), and Udr ("wave"). These daughters plagued the sailors and fishermen of the North Sea from the Scandinavian countries to Ireland. Ran and her daughters liked to create storms and disasters at sea. Ran would call up a violent storm, then watch her nine daughters dance wildly on the tops of the great waves. They continued to dance until ships were wrecked and sailors

drowned. Then Ran filled her nets with their human souls and took these souls back to her underwater cavern where she kept them in huge, tall silver and gold jars.

The god Heimdall, who guarded the Bifrost Bridge, was born from nine waves by an enchantment performed by the chief god Odin. Heimdall was called "the Son of Nine Waves," when Odin made the nine daughters of Ran his foster-mothers.

The nine daughters of Ran were also known in Ireland and recorded in the tale of Ruad, son of Rigdonn. This story links Ireland and Norway, for it was on a journey between the two countries that Ruad and his three ships ran into trouble with Ran's daughters. The three ships suddenly no longer moved through the water, but seemed to be held fast in the same position. Ruad dived into the cold seawaters to learn the reason for this and found himself facing the nine sea-giantess daughters of Ran, three easily holding one of his ships in place. These beautiful sea-women immediately seized him and carried him deep down in the ocean to their underwater palace.

Ruad made a bargain. If he willingly spent a night with each of the giantesses, they would allow him to return to his ships. As the giant sea-women returned him to his vessels nine days later, he was told that one of them would bear him a child. Eager to be on his way, Ruad promised to return to them after he finished his voyage to Norway.

After spending seven years in Norway, Ruad again set sail for home and headed straight toward Ireland. He had no intention of meeting Ran's nine daughters again and being stuck forever in their underwater palace. Besides, he did not really believe that his child had been born to one of them.

Suddenly, Ruad spotted the sea-giantesses coming after the ships, and a race began. With the wind filling his sails, and his skill of sailing a ship, Ruad was able to outrun Ran's daughters. As he turned to watch them one last time, he saw his giant child killed, and the head thrown at the ship. He hurried onward, without another backward glance.

Ran's daughters are far too unpredictable and malicious to work with or learn from. It is best to avoid them.

# Roane

The Gaelic word for "seal" is *roane*, although these beings are also called seal maidens. Traditional stories only speak of females, but perhaps those were the only ones to come ashore and be seen by humans. It is believed that these beings wear their sealskins just to travel through the seas, but look like humans without the skins. The roane are said to be the most gentle of all sea beings and will not even try for revenge against the seal hunters who kill their kin.

In the Scottish Highlands, the Orkneys, and Shetland Islands, the roane were known to come ashore, remove their sealskins, and dance in the moonlight on the northern shores. On occasion, a human fisherman would be brave enough to steal a skin, thus forcing the seal maiden to marry him. She would be a pleasant wife until she found her hidden sealskin. Then she escaped back to the sea.

A few of the descendants of these seal maiden marriages are born with a horny growth between their fingers. The MacCoddrums of the Seals are the most famous example.

Seal maidens are excellent to work with for music, dance, singing, and gaining love.

# Selkies

The Faroe Islands have another type of mermaid, called the seal-folk or selkies. These beings have a natural, humanlike form over which they wear a watertight sealskin. The skin is necessary for them to get from one underwater city to another, which as the tales tell, are enclosed in giant air bubbles, because the selkies are air-breathing creatures. The people of the Shetland Islands say that the selkies come ashore every ninth night. There they shed their sealskins and dance on the beaches in their human forms.

All of the selkies, male and female, are very beautiful and have large liquid-looking eyes. Female selkies will only stay with a human man if he steals her sealskin. As soon as she recovers it, she returns to the sea. The male selkies are very amorous beings, who often came ashore on the islands to court human women. However, they never remained in a relationship very long.

The ballad called *The Great Selkie of Sule Skerry* tells of a male selkie who has a child with a married human woman, but soon leaves her. Later, he overhears the woman's fisherman husband plotting to kill both her and the child. The selkie saves the woman and child by encasing them in sealskins and taking them under the sea to the city where he lives.

The offspring of mixed human and selkie couples always had webs between their fingers and/or toes. Frequently, this became a hereditary feature in a family.

Tradition in both Iceland and the Shetland Islands says that if a woman wants to bear a selkie child, she has to weep seven tears into the sea at night.

The selkies, however, are not like the gentle roane. Selkies will take vengeance on seal hunters by calling up great storms and sinking the boats. Thus, a selkie can help you learn storm magick.

# Tritons

The Tritons were mermen who followed the god Poseidon on his trips around the Mediterranean Sea. They look human down to their hips, but then have a forked fish tail. Although a few of their features are like other mermen, the Tritons are totally different. They have sharp teeth similar to those of fish. Their webbed fingers have long, sharp claws. Their hair is dark blue to blue-green. When they change their fish tails into legs so they can walk on land, it is easy to see the silvery scales and fins on their chests and bellies. This scale color turns to a silvery-blue on their legs.

The Tritons are the most malicious and mannerless of all the mermen. They play nasty tricks on seamen, both on the sea and on land. When not with Poseidon, they spend their time making human lives miserable whenever they can.

They do not fall in love with human women but are very lustful. They would gather in a gang and go into seaside towns, where they got drunk, raped any woman they saw, and vandalized everything in sight. The humans in these towns had to deal violently with these mermen—the only thing the Tritons seemed to understand.

At Tanagra, the people beheaded a Triton for the trouble he caused, and then erected a headless statue of a Triton to warn the others away.

The only real responsibility these creatures have is harnessing the dolphins to the chariot of Poseidon. They swim before him, blowing their conch shell horns to warn all to stay out of the way.

The father of all these Tritons is the ancient sea deity Triton. He is totally different from his unethical sons, being peaceful and helpful. A son of Poseidon, Triton had a human upper body, while his lower body was that of a dolphin. He was said to live in his deepwater palace near Libya, his favorite part of the Mediterranean. When seafarers found themselves in trouble from rough seas and storms, Triton emerged to blow his conch shell trumpet. This immediately calmed any storm. This god is also prophetic, and rides in a shell chariot drawn by sea-horses with crayfish claws for hooves.

It is safer to avoid working with the Tritons at all, however, one could learn prophecy from their father, Triton.

## Positive Water Creatures That Work With the Mer-Folk

### Dolphins or Porpoises

These intelligent sea creatures have long worked with the mer-folk. The dolphin is a small species of Cetacea, a category of aquatic mammals that include the whale. Dolphins are also friendly with humans, racing beside ships across the ocean waves.

Sailors believed that the presence of dolphins meant good weather and a lucky voyage. The audible sounds of the dolphins are a language that they use with each other and with the mer-folk. The dolphin was a sacred animal to many ancient cultures. In Greece, the dolphin was connected with the sun god Apollo, while the older Sumerians

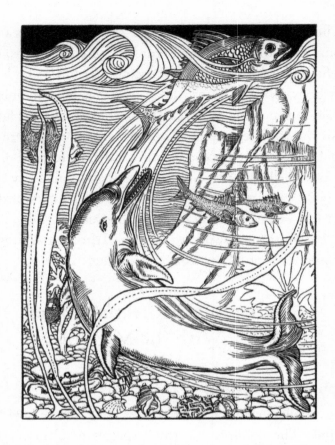

believed it was the animal of Astarte and Ishtar. In ancient Egypt, the dolphin was a symbol of the goddess Isis. Called "the King of Fishes" and "the Arrow of the Sea," they were connected with power and swiftness. Strangely enough, they were also considered to be the guides of souls into the Otherworld. Native Americans taught that they were keepers of the sacred breath of life.

Dolphins help the mer-teachers get across the ideas of eloquence, freedom, balance, and harmony. They can also teach humans to release intense emotions through breathing.

## Fish

Fish in general have been sacred to many love and fertility goddesses, particularly around the Mediterranean. A half-fish form was taken by such goddesses as Atargatis, Aphrodite, and Derceto. The Philistine god Dagon was also half fish.

The Celts believed that eating salmon and trout bestowed wisdom, healing, and the ability to prophesy. To the Chinese, the fish represents abundance and is connected with the goddess Kuan Yin.

Although the mer-folk eat certain fish, they also use the power of circling fish to build energy for their magick, just as they draw down energy from the stars at night.

## Hippocampus

This unusual sea creature has the front part of a horse, with the forelegs ending in powerful webbed fins, and a fish tail in the rear. Its mane is composed of scalloped fins. Very fine scales cover the foreparts of the hippocampus.

The name *hippocampus* means "sea-horse," but does not refer to the tiny seahorses that are more frequently seen. The

mer-folk like to ride these sea-steeds swiftly through the oceans. The carousing Tritons liked to ride the hippocampus. Sometimes the chariot of Poseidon/Neptune is pulled by dolphins, while at other times teams of hippocampus are used.

In meditations, the hippocampus is especially useful as an astral steed to move through other planes of existence seeking knowledge in dealing with emotional problems.

## Octopus

Usually found in all temperate and warm seas, there are about fifty species of octopi ranging in size from one inch to twenty-eight feet. They all have large eyes and eight tentacles with suction cups. Their jaws are sharp and look like beaks.

Paintings of the octopus have been found on jars in ancient temples. The Greeks and Minoans believed that this creature was connected with the sacred Goddess spiral—a line curving within itself until it reaches the Sacred Center and one of the earliest symbols linked with water deities and beings in the Mediterranean area.

The mer-folk use the black ink of the octopus in certain protection rituals. They also work with the suction power of the tentacles to add adherence to love spells.

## Salmon

Both the Atlantic and Pacific salmon were considered sacred and wise by many cultures in the northern latitudes. The mer-folk attach blessings for the rivers and land to the salmon as they migrate up the rivers for spawning. These spells gradually float off the fish as it passes a place that is in need of healing.

The mer-teachers can reveal how to attach blessing spells to certain fish, birds, and animals, so that the land and water blessings can be widely scattered.

## Seahorse

Mermaids love the antics and friendship of the tiny seahorses. They use the devotion and love of these creatures to add these qualities to certain spells, particularly those of love and friendship. Wearing a silver image of a seahorse will attract love and friendship to you.

## Sea-Lion

This fabulous creature is not the "sea lion" type of seal with which we are familiar. The sea-lion has the foreparts and maned head of a lion and the silvery back parts of a great fish. Although not especially dangerous, this creature should be treated with great care and respect. It has strong jaws, as well as clawed, webbed forefeet. The sea-lions like to live in packs along rocky shorelines. Its bellows can be heard for long distances underwater. Like the sea-pegasus, this creature is closely connected with the mer-folk.

## Tarroo-Ushtey

The Tarroo-Ushtey (pronounced *tar-oo ush-tar*) is a water bull found only on the Isle of Man. It is far less dangerous than the Cabyll-Ushtey and the Each Uisge; however, it is best to avoid contact with these creatures. (For more information on the Cabyll-Ushtey and Each Uisge, see Chapter 12.)

Although this sea creature looks like an ordinary bull, it has round ears and glittering eyes. It can never be tamed or captured. It is only seen when it comes out of the sea to graze on land with the ordinary cattle belonging to humans.

The Tarroo-Ushtey should be approached with extreme care, if at all. Its primary magickal use is as a guide during astral travels to the mer-folk.

## Whale

There are many different types of whales, ranging from 20 to 100 feet in length. They were considered to be powerful, magickal creatures by many ancient cultures. The singing and communication language of whales can be heard by other whales hundreds of miles away.

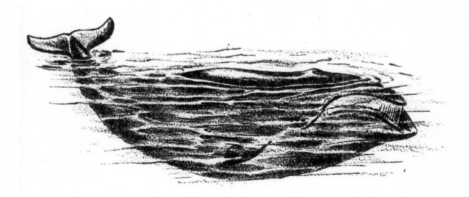

The mermaids love to ride the dolphins and whales, but they also respect them. They use the whales' ability to sing in such even, long notes to teach magickal chanting to human students.

## Winged Sea-Pegasus

Closely associated with the mer-folk, this creature is not the tiny seahorse we usually think of. The sea-pegasus has horse's hooves on its front legs and a horse's head and foreparts, but the back part is that of a giant fish.

Although we see pictures of this creature in Greek and Roman art, the Celts also knew of it. The Celtic god Manannan mac Lir harnessed winged sea-pegasus pairs to his sea chariot.

Winged sea-horses can help when a person needs to escape dangerous or limiting emotional problems.

# PART II

# The Water Folk

# CHAPTER 5

# Water Folk of
# the Elements

Undines and nymphs are the traditional Elemental spirits associated with the Element of Water. The Element of Water is
one of four Elements that are associated with the four cardinal
points, or directions. The word *undine* comes from the Latin
word *unda*, which means "wave" or "creatures of the waves."
Water in magick and ritual is the color blue, the emotions, and
the western direction of a circle.

It is more helpful to think of the Elements as states
of being, rather than physical conditions or actual beings.
Each Element has certain qualities, energies, natures, moods,
and magickal purposes. Each has positive and negative traits.
Because the forms of the Elements are only astral bodies, they
cannot be seen with the physical eyes, but only in meditation
or by clairvoyant vision or the inner eye.

However, the energy of the nymphs and undines can only be used in a Water Element situation. Elements cannot intrude into the force areas of other Elements. The Water Element beings can influence any type or action of physical water in all its forms. This includes rain, storms, hurricanes, tidal waves, and waterspouts (water tornadoes). They can also influence human emotions, because emotions fall under the Water Element's jurisdiction. To some degree, the subconscious mind can also be influenced by the Element of Water.

Those who are familiar with the tarot cards will recognize the Element of Water in the Minor Arcana suit of Cups. In the traditional descriptions of this particular suit of cards, you will find emotions in one form or another. The Cup cards cover the full range of human emotions, from love to hate.

However, there are other watery beings, along with the mer-folk, who also influence the Element of Water, particularly in magick and ritual. These are the tiny, nearly invisible creatures that live in the seas and fresh water. They are usually so small and transparent that we would fail to see them even

if they are put under a microscope. Their influence upon situations associated with the Element of Water, however, can be great if commanded correctly by humans taught by the mer-folk or the mer-folk themselves.

The magician, whether human or mer-folk, knows that to make magick work—and work quickly and well—she or he must find the exact point where applied pressure will change the balance of the universal energy only a little. This small change will affect the outcome of a situation, spell, desire, or event. The applied pressure is created by getting these tiny watery beings to all direct their energy at the focal spot while the magician performs the spell or ceremony. When massed together, the amount of energy produced by these creatures is much greater than one would expect.

Applying pressure at the vulnerable point is especially useful when working with weather. For example, if a hurricane is heading for land, a magician should try to turn it by small increments in a direction where it will do the least damage or perhaps even lose its force. Never try to turn a hurricane by applying force to the leading edge of the storm. This will be like locking horns with a bull. You will have no effect. First, you need to determine in which direction you want it sent. Then, you apply magickal energy to the wall of the hurricane eye that is farthest away from the approaching land.

Working the weather is very difficult and takes large amounts of your time in practice. You start with the basics of moving and splitting clouds. Next, you work on high and low pressure systems, followed by tiny changes in the jet stream. It is very rare for a human magician to have any effect on the jet stream at all.

You can use the same system of pressure points to move or disrupt negative ocean currents and sea movements. It is wise never to try moving major ocean currents, for they have a definite purpose of being where they are. However, you can disrupt or break the flow of such negative currents as El Niño and La Niña.

Although you can easily find the pressure point (an individual, a sequence in an event, an emotion, a decision) in ordinary magickal spells, learning to properly work weather or ocean currents can be a lifelong study.

Because the Water Element is connected with human emotions, you can call upon the undines for aid in helping people who are going through a bad emotional state. Do not recommend or use magick as the healing method. Suggest that the person talk to a therapist or doctor, if the emotional upset and behavior are bad enough. Water magick can help the person in small ways, but it is unable to reduce or control such emotional/mental health conditions as schizophrenia or bipolar disorder.

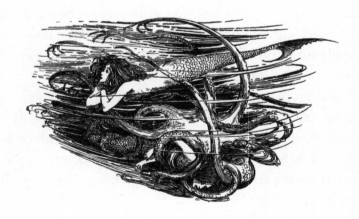

# CHAPTER 6

# Water Folk of Rivers

The mer-folk relatives who live in rivers are much like their ocean-going cousins. Some of them have human upper bodies and fish tails for the lower body parts. Others look totally human. All are human-sized. Most of these river beings have the malicious tendency to use their beauty and singing to attract sailors or other human men to a watery grave. Their favorite behavior is to sit on rocks along the riverbanks while they comb their long hair and sing.

The most famous of the river mermaids are the German lorelei. The composer Richard Wagner, in his opera *Das Rheingold*, has three Rhine Maidens singing along the Rhine River. In the *Niebelungen*, the lorelei are said to own and guard a magickal treasure that lies deep in the Rhine waters. The lorelei are also considered to be the guardians of magickal power and spiritual knowledge that lies deep within the subconscious mind of every human.

Old German stories portray the lorelei as beautiful women with fish tails who appear forever young. The songs they sing are so enchanting that they have lured many a ship to doom on the Rhine rocks. There is one specific rock in the Rhine that is named after the lorelei.

Although river mermaids exist everywhere, they are often not acknowledged or named. The only other culture to claim a specific river mermaid is Britain. This mermaid did not sit on the rocks and sing but used her Water magick instead. If she managed to swim three times around a ship, she could sink it.

The river mermaids, particularly the lorelei, are adept at teaching the magickal uses of the voice and chanting. They

Magickal Mermaids & Water Creatures

will also help any human who searches for ancient spiritual knowledge.

The Nixies, another form of river mer-folk, are found in German springs and rivers. They are called the Nickers in Iceland. They are quite similar to the Greek Nereids. The mother of the Nixies is a Chaos Goddess, called Nott by the Norse and Nyx by the Greeks; both names mean "Mother Night." The Nixies and Nereids have the task of collecting the human souls of the dead and taking them into the Otherworld, where the souls wait to be reincarnated.

The male Nixies are rarely seen by humans. Both sexes of Nixies are humanoid in shape, with lightly scaled greenish skin. Although they have no fish tails, they do have webbed fingers and toes. Their hair is either green or a silver blonde, while they have silver or silver-tinted blue eyes.

Female Nixies like to lie or sit along the riverbanks and sun themselves. They admire themselves in the water while they comb their long hair and sing. If they hear a human approach, they quickly slide back into the river.

The female Nixies are very adept at casting love spells. Handsome young men have to beware walking along river-banks, or the Nixies will lure them into the river with love spells. Then they enslave them deep in their river lair, never to be seen again.

The only protection humans have against Nixies is metal. Exposure to any kind of metal will make a Nixie powerless, and if exposed to the metal too long, it will kill the water being. This is why many German fishermen kept a knife stuck in the bottom of their boat on the inside. Metal was, therefore, readily available.

Scandinavia, Estonia, and Latvia have similar beings, which they call Neckan, Necker, Nakki, or Neck. These beings are masters of shapeshifting, playing the harp, and singing. They spend their time along the shores of rivers and lakes, where they try to entice humans into the water so they can drown them.

Although the Nixies are tricky and not to be much trusted, they are adept at love spells, learning to play stringed instruments, and magickal singing or chanting.

The Russian and Slavic people have water maidens called the Rusalka (singular) or Rusalki (plural). They do not seem to have just one distinct appearance or typical behavior; these change from place to place in Russia and the other surrounding cultures. There is one type of Rusalki in northern Russia and another type in the south.

All Rusalki are extremely dangerous and mischievous whenever humans are around rivers in the summer. During the winter months, these creatures live deep in the water, under the ice. However, at Rusalki Week, when summer arrives, the Rusalki have the power to leave the water and go into the surrounding forests.

The Slavic people believed that when Rusalki Week came, these creatures climbed up the slim willow branches or birch trees that hung over the water. When moonlight filled the forest at night, they swung on the branches and called to each other. Often, the Rusalki would slip down the trees and dance in clearings. Sometimes, they even used a farmer's fields as a dancing ground. The southern Slavs said that one could tell where the Rusalki danced because the grass was thicker and the wheat more abundant.

In northern Russia, the Rusalki look like naked, drowned women. They appear cadaverous with eyes that shine with an evil green fire. They wait along the streams for travelers, then drag their victim deep under the water, where they torture and drown them.

The Rusalki of southern Russia have a totally different appearance. They take the form of beautiful, young, human maidens with moonlight-pale faces. They wear very sheer garments, meant to entice human males. The Rusalki would stand in the edge of a river, wringing out their long hair and singing sweetly to their victim. As soon as the man waded into the water after them, they pushed him under and drowned him.

Along the Rhine River, which flows for miles through Russia, Austria, and Germany, these beings were called the vila. They are different in both appearance and behavior from the lorelei who primarily inhabit the German waters. The vila are also found along the Danube and Dnieper Rivers. The Danube ones are described as gracious and beautiful, while those of the

Dnieper are said to be wicked, unattractive females with uncombed hair. Those of both the Dnieper and Danube sing enchanting songs unknown to their cousins in northern Russia.

The Rusalki, as a group, had other bad habits, besides drowning people. On a whim, they could ruin a harvest with heavy rains. They also liked to tear up fishnets they found in the streams and to destroy dams and water mills. Some of them even stole clothes, linen, and thread from human women.

A traveler could protect her- or himself against the Rusalki and vila by carrying a few leaves of wormwood (Artemisia absinthium). People sprinkle this herb on anything that these creatures might steal or destroy. If a stream or pond got infested badly with Rusalki or vila, great quantities of wormwood were sprinkled on the waters.

The Rusalki and vila are far too dangerous for a magician to become involved with.

# CHAPTER 7

# Water Folk of Small Streams and Waterfalls

Ancient philosophers and magicians believed that some form of the water folk lived in every spring, fountain, creek, river, lake, fen or marsh, waterfall, and ocean. They also knew of the undines that only work with the Element of Water, and they were aware that these other water beings were similar, yet different, in appearance and in their magickal abilities.

The tinier versions of the mer-folk that live in smaller bodies of water—such as fountains, springs, and slow-moving creeks—look somewhat like humans, but in their infant stage look more like sea mermaids.

The mer-folk adults of these smaller bodies of water are very tiny, human-shaped beings. Their iridescent scales flash beautiful colors in the sunlight. Their children begin life looking almost like tadpoles. They have a human-looking upper body and a fish tail that disappears when they reach adulthood. They have to stay in water until the transformation is completed.

The older beings of this group are humanlike, with arms and legs. They have the ability to propel themselves swiftly along slow-moving creeks, up fountain spray, and in and out of springs. They love to dance in and on the water like faeries. However, they do not have wings or fins. Like all mer-folk, the adults love to sun themselves along the edges of their watery homes. They also like to sing and chant. They are extremely shy around humans, but if one is patient and gentle, it is possible to coax them to teach you water divination.

The water beings who live in waterfalls look much like their close cousins in the fountains and smaller water sources. The only exception is that the size of their human-shaped bodies is determined by the size of the waterfall. Therefore, their size can range from very small to human size. These waterfall folk have the ability to flash straight up the falling water and then drift downward, twisting and leaping through the water and spray. Their children begin life with a fish tail, which disappears when they become adults. Until then, the young ones must play in the pools at the bottom of the waterfalls.

The homes of water folks are formed of moss and nearby small vegetation if they are in creeks, waterfalls, and springs. However, the ones associated with fountains build small, nearly invisible homes near their fountain so they can be near their children, who must stay in the water. On occasions when the fountain becomes dry, these little water folk will burrow into nearby areas of mud to hibernate until the fountain flows again. If their fountain becomes permanently damaged and dry, they will enlist the aid of birds to carry them to another appropriate spot where they start a new life.

The water folk in waterfalls live among the rocks and moss behind the fall itself. All water folk survive cold weather, snow, and ice by hibernating at the bottom of their watery home. The waterfall folk rarely help humans at all. However, they do possess great healing knowledge.

In Germany, there is a water being associated with small waterfalls, who is found nowhere else. This is the *stromkarl*, or river-man. He has a beautiful enchanting voice and plays wonderful, sad music on his harp. He dresses in colorful native clothing. His music is usually heard only at night. He is not fond of human company but will tolerate those who are sincere in their study of Water magick. He has the ability to teach one how to sing magickal songs and notes.

# CHAPTER 8

# Water Folk of the Desert and Arid Regions

Although most people would not think of mer-folk living in arid, desert regions, they can be found there. The small watery places where native animals drink is sparsely inhabited by water folk. Even the alkaline pools have their inhabitants, who definitely are not human-friendly and are colored to match the poisonous water.

These relatives of the mer-folk are the smallest of all the species, being less than two inches tall. Instead of the blues and iridescence usually found coloring the mer-folk, the desert water beings have scales that are usually a muddy brown color, which makes them invisible to human eyes. They also have tiny fish tails like the ocean mermaids and can lay aside their skin to walk on the land. However, because the areas these beings inhabit are so hot, they hide in the water all day, coming out only at night. Their magickal powers are based on learning to improvise and using what is around you for your magick.

The water folk are also found in desert oases. This type of mermaid is a shapeshifter of great ability, changing from minnow-to human-size in the blink of an eye. They do not have fish tails, but have a humanlike form. Their scales are so tiny that they look as if they have been dusted with powdered gold and silver. They have dark eyes and very black hair. This makes their skin seem even paler and more sparkly. They are strongly family-oriented and love children. They built their homes close to the water, but under the trees. These little houses are made out of nearby native materials.

One of their greatest joys is to dance up magick under the moonlight. Sometimes a traveler is fortunate enough to hear the faint sounds of their drums and instruments.

These beings are gifted with the powers of granting wishes, protecting travelers who stop at an oasis, healing humans and animals through the water in their homes, and sending love to lonely people. The oases water folk become unhappy when lonely humans come into their areas. They understand that love is the greatest healer of all and can direct lives onto positive paths.

Call upon the oases water folk during meditations on healing, universal love, and finding the perfect love to share your life. This type of mer-folk loves to help humans create better physical, emotional, and spiritual lives.

Magickal Mermaids & Water Creatures

# CHAPTER 9

# Water Folk of the Swamps, Fens, and Wetlands

It should be no surprise to readers that there is even a type of mer-folk who lives in the dripping, foggy marshes, swamps, and fens. Although they are humanlike in outward appearance, with arms and legs, they are thin and cadaverous looking, as if they are diseased and half dead. They have the usual mer-folk webs between their fingers and toes and are covered with tiny scales all over their bodies. Like a few of the ocean mer-folk, they also have sharp teeth and fish-like eyes. Their dark, stringy hair looks like dead, water-slimed pieces of weed and grass. The odor of rotting vegetation clings to their bodies.

These beings usually appear only at night or on foggy, cloudy days. They do not like sunlight or humans who drain their moist, watery homes to make way for construction. They are the most unpredictable and tricky of the smaller mer-folk. They will deliberately lead humans astray in the fog by making their bodies give off a faint glow like a dim flashlight, and they will put mossy slime into equipment overnight, causing humans to have trouble running the machines.

However, the Marsh Mermaids care for the animals that live in their swamps, fens, and wetlands. They try to protect the other creatures from unfriendly humans and predatory or savage animals.

They can amplify their voices, often at extreme ranges. One may either hear a very high-pitched keening or a deep, threatening grumble coming from these unfriendly moist areas of land late at night.

If part of their land is left undisturbed, but part of it is used for building houses, the swamp folk will quickly try to frighten or play tricks on the humans occupying these houses. Usually, their first victims are children, because human children are most likely to see them. These cadaverous looking mer-folk

Magickal Mermaids & Water Creatures

hang on the windowsill and peer in until they catch a human's attention or make them feel their presence. Then they make hideous faces or amplify the human's secret fears until everyone in the house is uneasy. They play tricks such as putting moss slime into any piece of mechanical machinery. Sometimes, when enough of them join together, they cause different molds to grow on the inside walls of the house.

Mer-folk of the swamps, fens, and wetlands are extremely unfriendly to humans and should not be approached at all.

# CHAPTER 10

# Lake Mermaids

There is a very long history of lake folk, particularly lake maidens. They look the most like humans of all the mer-folk. These maidens do not have fish tails. The slight webs between their fingers and toes are difficult to see at all, and they rarely have scales anywhere on their bodies. Except for a remote pale beauty, their faces are completely humanlike. They are so much at home in both water and on land that they often live among humans for some time, without anyone guessing their true identity. They know powerful magick. However, one must take care to avoid their glamour spells when working with them. These spells are capable of enticing a human into the maiden's lake forever.

Lake maidens are even found in the folklore of Spain, where they are called the water maidens. These small, human-shaped beings dwell in lakes, ponds, and pools all over the country of Spain. Each of them has a star on her forehead, but no fish tail. They also do not have the usual webbed fingers and toes; their fingers and feet look like any human's fingers or feet. Their bodies shimmer with the iridescent shine of golden scales, although no scales have ever been associated with the water maidens. Their golden hair almost reaches their feet. Each of them wears white rings, while on their left wrists they wear a gold band with black stripes.

The Spanish water maidens spend most of their time in their lakes or pools. When they do come out to walk through the meadows, everywhere they step, bright yellow flowers spring up. Any human who finds these special yellow flowers will be blessed with happiness.

The water maidens have a very powerful gift. They can affect and change the way things are or the way events appear to be moving. In other words, they have a special talent for changing the future.

Wales has many stories of sinister beings and creatures. However, they also have a story associated with a particular family that has to do with kind lake maidens, known in Welsh as the Gwragedd Annwn (pronounced *gwrageth anoon*). The lake maidens have a complete human form, are very beautiful, and sometimes consent to marry mortals. Like most other mer-folk, the maidens liked to comb their long hair while walking along the banks of their watery home.

One of the earliest recorded stories about the lake maidens has to do with the Lady of Llyn y Fan Fach, which is a small lake near the Black Mountains in Wales. Sometime in the 12th century, a young farm lad from Blaensawde, near Mydfai, was walking near the lake when he saw a maiden. As he watched her comb out her golden hair, he fell in love with her. In a short time, he convinced her to marry him. However, his new wife warned him that he could never hit her, even in jest. For if he hit her three times, she would return to her lake.

The couple lived happily for many years during which the lady bore her husband three sons. But the man forgot her warning, and on three occasions gave her a love tap. On the last tap, the lady turned without a word, left the house, and returned to her lake. No amount of pleading from her husband would cause her to see or speak with him.

However, when the three boys were alone, their mother would come to see them. She taught them the deep secrets of medicine. All three boys became the famous physicians of Mydfai. This skill in medicine descended in the family until the bloodline died out in the 19th century.

The Lady of the Lake, in the stories of King Arthur, is obviously a lake maiden. Giving the unique sword to Arthur was symbolic of passing on magickal knowledge to a person who had earned it. It was also the fulfilling of destiny or karma.

There is another type of lake being that is rarely seen and about which little is known. These very tiny beings can also

be found in small, slow-moving creeks and gentle waterfalls that empty into lakes. They are extremely shy about being seen by humans and avoid all communication with them. Some make their little homes among the reeds along river-banks and lake-shores, while others live in magickal bubbles on the underside of lily pads. Still others make homes in small crevices and caves among the rocks at the bottom of the waterfalls. Sometimes these waterfall homes are composed of moss, a tangle of reeds and cattails, and strategically placed rocks.

One can safely work with lake maidens as long as care is taken not to be captivated by their beauty. Males must particularly take care that this does not happen. Lake maidens will help you to see your destiny or karma of this lifetime. Some of them are experts in healing, while others can fill your life with happiness.

# PART III

# Connections, Warnings, and Power

# CHAPTER 11

# The Connection Between Dragons, Faeries, and the Mer-Folk

Magicians who can cross into the astral realms to talk with and learn from their special teachers know that all the creatures and beings who move between the astral realm and Earth can work together if necessary. Each species has its own special ways of working magick and different magickal energies. When all the species consult together and deem it necessary, they will work together to solve problems or create a manifestation or earthly event.

The dragons, faeries, and mer-folk are only a few of those that dwell on the astral plane, but they are the most likely to work together on magickal projects that will benefit a human. Dragons represent Fire and Air Elements. Faeries, who spend much of their time in our plane of existence, are of Earth and Air Elements, while the mermaids represent Water and Earth Elements.

All three of these species also have developed long histories of interacting with humans. They are the most active today with humans, strengthening old ties and creating new ones that will reap benefits in the future for the astral creatures and humans alike.

Two of the most important statements taught to human magicians by these three astral species should be remembered by all. First: some things must be believed to be seen. Second: anything a person believes in strongly enough will manifest or come into physical reality.

Although this book deals primarily with the mer-folk and water creatures, if you are determined enough to learn all the magick you can, you might want to branch out your studies into the realms of dragons and faeries.

Practice the following meditation several times until you are comfortable with the mer-person who comes as your teacher.

## Calling a Mer-Folk Teacher

Begin your meditation as described in Chapter 3: Sit in a comfortable chair with your hands in your lap and your feet flat on the floor. Make certain you will not be disturbed by the telephone, someone at the door, pets, or any other people in the house.

Visualize a brilliant white light surrounding and penetrating your body. This is your protection throughout the meditation. Now, slowly begin to relax your body, beginning at the feet and ending at the head.

After you are relaxed and surrounded by white light, visualize yourself sitting on a beach or a lakeshore near the water. Mentally call out your need for a merperson to come to you as a teacher in your study of Water magick. Wait quietly, for it may take a few moments to receive an answer from the right teacher for you.

At last you see a trail of ripples and bubbles coming toward you from the body of water you are facing. Suddenly, a merperson stands up and walks or slides toward you through the shallow water. You may be given a mermaid, merman, or lake maiden as your first teacher. Other teachers will be added as needed in the future.

Your teacher sits down beside you and introduces herself (or himself). She looks at the palms of your hands, runs her

damp hands carefully over the crown of your head, and looks deep into your eyes as she asks if you are ready to learn Water magick. When you answer yes, she begins to tell you about the very elementary steps in learning this special magick and the responsibilities that go with it.

She asks you to cup your hands together and close your eyes. She pours water into your hands and asks you if it is fresh or salt water. She will continue this until you learn to feel the difference. Then she will repeat the exercise, but include water from lakes, streams, waterfalls, and swamps. When you have learned the difference in the feel of these waters, your teacher asks you to become more aware of all the types of water that surrounds you on the Earth plane.

As she prepares to leave, she hands you a basket of seashells. You will be taught how to use these different shells in Water magick. She quickly slides back into the water and disappears. You think of your physical body, and slide down a tunnel of light into it. You open your eyes. The meditation is ended. (For more information about meditation, see Chapter 14.)

# CHAPTER 12

# Dangerous Water Folk

There are sea and water creatures that are far too dangerous for any magician to become involved with. They are listed here so that you will recognize them, should you see them during your explorations with the mer-folk.

If you come upon one of these creatures during your astral travels or in meditations or dreams, call upon your teachers at once. While he or she is rapidly coming to help, throw up a shield of white light between the creature and yourself. You must be aware at all times and learn to feel the vibrations of these negative astral creatures before they get close to you. If you detect them first and surround yourself with extra white light, they will not be able to see or find you.

# Ahuizotl

In the highland lakes of Central America lives a strange water monster. Its description is very vague and unreliable because few who see it survive. The ahuizotl considers all the fish in its lake to belong to it, and resents fishermen who "steal" them by net and hook. When it becomes aware of a fisherman, it angrily lashes its long tail on the water, causing terrible storms. At times, the ahuizotl has been known to tip over boats and drown the fishermen.

# Aughisky

Sea-horses called the aughisky (pronounced *agh-iski*) were once so plentiful in the Highlands that they frequently left the sea to gallop over the fields. This usually occurred in early November. When they came ashore, they frequently devoured cattle on the moors. Tradition says that if a person could get the sea-horse away from the water and get a bridle and saddle on it, it made a wonderful horse. However, if it so much as glimpsed the sea, the rider could not stop it from

plunging into the ocean. Unless the rider jumped free, the aughisky would eat him.

## Bunyips

Bunyips are rarely seen water monsters found in Australia. They are also known as kine pratie, wowee wowee, tunatabah, and dongus. There seem to be several different species of this creature, who all live in swamps and marshes in different areas. Some of them have a fish tail and a flat face like a bulldog, while others have a very long neck with a beaked head like an emu. A few have the flowing mane of a sea serpent, and some even resemble humans. Bunyips can quickly be identified by their hideous faces and the fact that their feet are turned backward.

These unfriendly creatures build their dens in the banks of rivers, water holes, or mangrove swamps. As their dens begin to dry out in summer, the bunyips burrow deep into the mud and hibernate. They become very active during and after long periods of rain. It is then that their strange booming voices can be heard for long distances. They are never heard during a drought.

## Cabyll-Ushtey

The Isle of Man knew of a different sea-horse called the Cabyll-Ushtey. It was pale gray, very dangerous, and liked human flesh.

# Each Uisge

The most dangerous of all the water horses is the Highland Each Uisge (pronounced *ech-oosh-kya*). This vicious creature haunts the sea and lochs of northern Scotland. The Each Uisge will appear in the form of a sleek horse, teasing humans to ride it. If a human does mount it, they are unable to dismount. The sea-horse then races straight into the loch or sea with the rider. There, it eats all of the human except the liver.

# Kappa

In Japan, they have a very malicious creature—a demon dwarf—called a kappa. Kappas are only found in Japanese seas, rivers, or ponds. He looks like a grotesque, naked, furless monkey-man. He is the size of a child and wears a tortoise shell on his back. His fingers and toes have claws and are webbed. His skin has a greenish tint, and he always smells pungently of rotten fish.

His round, evil eyes peer over a sharply beaked nose. The most important part of a kappa is a circular depression on the crown of his head.

The kappa lies in wait near his watery home for people or animals to stray close enough to capture. With his liking for blood, he consumes his victim from the inside out.

There are only two ways to escape from a kappa. One is to bow politely to him. He will bow in return, which will spill the water from the depression on his head. This leaves him powerless until he refills the spot with water. This gives the victim time to escape. The second method is to carve the name of each family member into a cucumber and throw it into the Kappa's watery home. This keeps the named people safe for a year, after which the ritual must be repeated.

## Kelpies

There is a creature known in both Scotland and Cornwall. It can assume many forms, but mostly appears as a white horse with a foamy-looking mane. Just before a storm strikes, the kelpies wail loudly.

The kelpie often appears by a riverbank as a young horse wearing a bridle. If a person is quick enough to exchange the bridle for an ordinary one, the kelpie has to work for the human. However, it should never be overworked or kept too long, lest it place a curse on the human and all family descendants.

If a human does mount the kelpie and doesn't exchange the bridle, it immediately leaps into the nearest deep water and nearly drowns the human before he or she can get off.

## Kraken

The kraken is sometimes confused with the giant octopus, when in reality it is an entirely different creature. The Scandinavian sailors knew it to be a terrible sea menace. It is far bigger than a sperm whale. This giant creature prefers to stay in the waters of the North Atlantic and along the coast of Norway.

Sometimes when it floats on the ocean waters, its body is mistaken for an island. It is so large and powerful that it can drag a man off a ship or crush the ship itself. Sailors kept a

lookout for unusual boiling activity in the waters around them when sailing through certain areas. This boiling water look was a signal that a kraken was rising to the surface. Once it did, there was no escape from its powerful, deadly attack.

There are two distinct, recorded reports of krakens in Norwegian coastal towns. One report, dated 1680 C.E., says that a young kraken got wedged in the narrow channel of Altstahong. No one dared try to help it get loose, so the creature finally died. As the corpse rotted, a horrid odor filled the town. It got so bad before the body washed out to sea that the villagers were afraid they would catch a terrible disease from it. Again in 1752, the Norwegian Bishop Pontoppidan was aboard a ship when they saw a kraken. The bishop wrote that the black ink from this creature blackened the seas around the ship for some distance.

Ireland has stories of a similar sea monster that they call an Orc. This creature kept ravaging an island off the coast of Ireland until a Saracen knight finally managed to kill it.

# Nokke

A Danish water spirit, called the nokke, can live in both fresh and salt water. His head, chest, and arms are human, but the rest of his body is that of a horse, much like the land-dwelling centaur. He is very handsome, with gold ringlets in his hair, and wearing a red cap. During the summer months, the nokke likes to sit on the water at night and play his harp.

There are a few tales of nokkes falling in love with human women, but this was dangerous, for he would take his love back into the water with him.

Nokkes are repelled by steel or iron, which is why fisherman and other water travelers put a knife or a nail in the bottom of the boat.

# The Sirens

Alchemists of medieval times perpetuated the image of sirens as double-tailed mermaids, although they are actually human-birds. The Greek sirens are associated with the ocean and water, because they sat on great rocks along the ocean shore, played their lyres, and sang love songs. Their voices enchanted sailors who would jump from their ships and drown. The sirens had a taste for human flesh as well.

At one time, the sirens had been river nymphs, children of the river god Achelous and the nymph Calliope. For some small infraction, they were turned into human-birds by the goddess Ceres.

## Vodyanoi

The name *vodyanoi* seems to cover several types of Russian monsters that liked to live in mill ponds and pools. However, each type lived the same length of time. They were born on the new moon, aged as the moon waxed, and died at the full moon, to be reborn at the next new moon.

The vodyanoi have several different appearances. These change from place to place, thus leading to the theory of several species using the same basic name. Some look like old men with green hair and beards, which get whiter as the moon gets fuller. Sometimes they take the form of beautiful, naked women with green hair. As the moon ages, they become wrinkled and old. One has to be careful of floating logs in Russia. It might be a vodyanoi in disguise. Another form is a giant fish covered with moss and water weeds. At night it is most likely to appear as a snarling monster with great, fiery eyes.

# CHAPTER 13

# Earth Power in
# Water Magick

The Elements of Earth and Water frequently combine natu-
rally, sometimes for positive things, other times for negative
occurrences. This chapter will teach you several methods of
combining Earth and Water for magickal results. You will also
learn to dowse for natural underground lines of water, which
are similar to the energy lines called ley lines. In fact, if you
are fortunate to find a ley line, you can use the power of that
energy line to charge jars of water for magickal workings.

All it takes to dowse with a pendulum or L-bars is practice
and self-confidence. Pendulums on a short chain are easy to purchase in New Age shops or online. To make L-bars, clip the
hanger part off two metal clothes hangers and bend a handle at
one end of the wire long enough for you to comfortably hold.
Straighten the remaining wire extending out from the handle
and cut to about eighteen inches, or whatever length feels right
to you.

The pendulum will signal a ley line or underground water stream by circling rapidly when you walk across it. When using the L-bars, hold one in each hand loosely by the handles, with the long ends pointed straight out in front of you. When you walk across an energy line or underground stream, the L-bars will quickly flip over each other.

If using a pendulum, one has to remember that body motion can affect the movement. Therefore, the dowser should walk slowly and stop frequently to see how the pendulum reacts.

When dowsing a piece of ground, you need to be certain if and just where there are buried power, water, telephone, and/ or sewer lines. Your pendulum or L-bars will react to these in much the same way that they react to ley lines and underground streams. It is wise to have small wooden stakes or little wires with colorful cloth tied to them to mark the places where you have dowsing reactions. Using this technique, you are less likely to forget exactly where your dowsing tools indicated underground lines.

When actually dowsing, you must keep in mind what you are dowsing for. For example, if you seek underground streams, that is what you must think about, and only that. If you allow your mind to dwell on both underground streams and ley lines at the same time, you will get inaccurate, confused results.

To discover in which direction the line goes, you will need to dowse across where you think it leads in several different places. Some lines are perfectly straight, while others may be straight for a time, then meander briefly in another direction.

Although we usually only hear of ley lines being in Britain, they are actually all over the planet. It is also common for underground streams of water to flow along or very close to these energy lines.

A power spot is a place where two or more of these lines meet. When this happens, it is called a sacred place. The pendulum will circle so fast when held over this spot that it will become almost parallel to the earth. The L-bars will cross so far over each other that you may have them slap against your body. If water bubbles to the surface at this intersecting point, it is known as a holy spring or well.

The reason for trying to find these lines is that you can set out jars of water along a ley line during a full moon. This will fill the water with Earth energy that is very useful in magick. This water, when mixed with a little sea salt, can be lightly sprinkled through a house to purify the vibrations, or sprinkled clockwise in a circle in which you plan to do magick. This contains the energy you raise until you are ready to release it to manifest; this happens when you "cut" across the circle's edge with your hand. It can also be  sprinkled on a sick person to help increase the other healing powers being used. When sprinkled across tarot cards, runes, or other divinatory tools, this sacred water will increase the ability to get a more accurate reading of a question or the future.

Either holy water (water charged in the full moon, as described previously) or ordinary water can be mixed with a little soil for other magickal purposes also. You can mix one teaspoon of water with a tablespoon of soil; pour this mixture over an underground water line and write the name of a sick person into this mud. Chant:

*May this mixture of earth and water bless and purify*
*[person's name].*

Leave the mixture on the ground until time or rain obliterates it.

You can mix a much thinner mixture of charged water and soil and use it to pour over the top of the soil of your houseplants. It is also helpful to use this type of mixture when working with a plant that isn't doing very well.

If you live along the coast, or go there for a visit, you have a great opportunity to work simple but powerful Water magick. Meditate and ask for the aid of your mer-teacher to see which quality or desire would benefit you most at the moment. Then, as the tide is beginning to come in, walk as far as is safe out on the sand. Using your finger or a small stick, write on the sand that which you desire, such as prosperity, a new job, love, good health, reconciliation, spiritual growth, or whatever you have decided you need. As the tide comes in, it will dissolve your writing and carry the vibrations of your desire straight to the mer-folk in the ocean. It is rather like sending a letter or telegram. If possible, repeat this for three consecutive days.

If it is at all possible, set out jars along an energy or water line when it is raining. Then cap them and leave them on the line for at least three days to charge them with greater energy. If unable to do this, another powerful source is to get jars of springwater—after asking the resident mer-folk's permission, of course. Jars of water drawn from the tap should sit on the line for at least a week. Some well water, depending upon its purity, may need to stay there for five days. The ultimate water to use, however, is seawater.

# PART IV

# Rituals for Mermaids and Water Folk

# CHAPTER 14

# Water Magick Meditations

To learn the concentration necessary for casting spells, it is a good idea to start with meditations. The same type of visualization is required for both meditation and spells. You must be able, in your mind, to see each astral movement and step you make and the end result when you are finished. Therefore, I am including several meditations with these techniques in mind, which will become harder and more elaborate as you work your way through them. This visualization and concentration work will prepare you for performing any of the spells in Chapter 15.

Whenever you do any of the meditations explained in this chapter, first prepare with the following activities, as we touched on in Chapter 3. Sit in a comfortable chair with your hands in your lap and your feet flat on the floor. Make certain you will not be disturbed by the telephone, someone at the door, pets, or any other people in the house. It may be helpful to play a CD of the quiet sound of waves, to mask any slight background noises. If you put each meditation on a tape, leave spaces in the appropriate places so that you have time to explore or listen to whoever is speaking to you.

Visualize a brilliant white light surrounding and penetrating your body. This is your protection throughout the meditation. Now, slowly begin to relax your body, beginning at the feet and ending at the head. During this time, breathe steadily and evenly.

## Making Sea Friends Meditation

Visualize yourself lying or sitting on a warm, sandy beach, watching the movement of the waves as they make their way to shore. Then, you see dolphins jumping in and out of the water, just beyond the shallow shoreline. One of the dolphins looks straight at you and begins to swim toward you. You wade out into the water to meet this wonderful creature. It looks up at you with smiling eyes and chatters in its clicking, high-pitched sounds. Gently, you reach down to stroke its shining back. The dolphin chatters again, pushing against your legs, until you are facing the wide expanse of open ocean. You realize that the dolphin wants you to hold on to its dorsal fin and let it lead you somewhere special. You grasp the upright fin in both hands as you squat beside this sea mammal. Quickly, the powerful dolphin pulls you out into the ocean, with the rest of the dolphins surrounding you.

You have no fear of the water and find you can easily breathe under or out of the sea. It is a marvelous feeling as you streak through the waves with your dolphin escort. Now you see mermaids and mermen join the dolphins. Your dolphin rolls over in a spin, and you go with it, laughing in wonder and joy.

Soon, you hear a strange sound reverberating through the water. Its notes are slow and drawn out, yet like very beautiful chanting in tones, rather than words. The dolphins and mer-folk head directly toward the sound. Soon another similar sound joins the first, combining in a strange harmony. Ahead, you see a monstrous dark gray shape in the water. It is a whale. The whale is making the musical sounds.

Your dolphin swims close to the whale so you can reach out and run your hand down its smooth skin. You are so close that the whale's singing vibrates through your head.

All the dolphins and mer-folk swim to the surface, forming a large circle around the giant sea mammal. The whale surfaces and calmly watches the sea creatures around it. When one of the mermen raises a hand in a salute, the whale dives, smacking its huge flukes on the surface just before disappearing. Water splashes everywhere, and the dolphins give a funny little chattering laugh.

A mermaid shouts a warning and points toward a dorsal fin cutting through the water toward the group. It is a shark. Three of the dolphins swim straight at the shark, ramming it with their noses in a specific spot on the shark's body. Soon, the shark floats dead in the water.

"The shark was intent upon attack," one of the mermaids says, as she swims to your side. "We could not turn it aside, so the dolphins used what nature gave them: the ability to kill the shark by ramming it's vulnerable spot. Come. I have other sea creatures for you to meet."

The mermaid leads the way deeper into the sea, and your dolphin follows her. In the sunlit water ahead, you see several octopi leisurely floating, their long tentacles waving with the motion of the water. The mermaid gently closes her hand around a very small one and returns to you with it. She puts her hand against your arm and then moves it away. Clinging to your arm is a very small octopus, no more than three inches long. You can feel the gentle suction of the cups on its tentacles as it moves around your arm. Suddenly, the octopus propels itself away from you, leaving behind a tiny cloud of ink in the ocean.

The mermaid smiles as she guides your dolphin toward a cliff that runs deep into the ocean. Clinging to this cliff are mussels and starfish. Little groups of seahorses swim back and forth with the groups of various fish. The mussel shells are open, drawing in tiny particles of food. When you touch one of the shells, it snaps shut in self-defense.

The mermaid and your dolphin head back toward the beach where you started your journey. You pat the dolphin good-bye as you stand in the shallow water. It swims quickly away to join the others. The mermaid, however, joins you on the rocks of the tidal pools along the beach. She points out the

Magickal Mermaids & Water Creatures

little crabs, anemones, and other sea life that exists in these small pools.

"There is magick in everything on Earth," she says as she sits beside you. "Since the first life on this planet evolved from the seas, water contains the most magick. If a magician is to be truly powerful, they must learn the secrets of Water magick and the power of self-control of the emotions. Do you wish to continue your studies?"

You answer yes. The mermaid takes your left hand and fastens a bracelet of silver and gold bands around your wrist.

"This sign will let all water beings know that you are a true student in Water magick. Beware of the ones you know to be unreliable. The others will help you to learn what they know. Although some knowledges are small and seem insignificant, they have their purpose and place in Water magick."

She slides back into the water and waves good-bye before disappearing under the waves. You sit for a moment and contemplate all the creatures you saw in the ocean and how everything worked in the pattern for which it was designed. Then you think of your physical body. You slide down the tunnel of light into that body. You open your eyes. The meditation is finished.

## Mermaids of Waterfalls and Streams Meditation

Visualize yourself walking along a small stream near a forest. You listen to the babble of the stream as it makes its way around and over small stones in the streambed. In one hand you carry a small pouch in which are tiny bits of crystal.

You see a tiny quick movement in the water in a pool on the downside of a stone, where the water pours over the rock, making a miniature waterfall. You kneel down to look closer. At first you think the creatures swimming in the shade of the stone are tadpoles. But there is an iridescent flash of scales in the sunlight, and tadpoles do not have scales. You look closer and see the pale flash of a human-looking upper body on these tiny creatures. They are a type of baby mermaid that is found in small streams. Then you see a completely formed, human-looking adult ride the water down the miniscule waterfall. The adult gently herds the young ones into the shadow of the stone where they are less likely to be seen.

"I won't hurt you," you think at the tiny mer-folk.

You search through the crystal pieces in the pouch until you find three that are so small you can barely see them. Gently, you let them fall into the middle of the stream, hoping the mer-folk will later accept your offering.

You continue your walk until the small stream joins a large river. You follow this into a higher, very rocky place. You hear the loud roar of a tall waterfall. When you round a turn of the river, obscured by trees, you can see the falls ahead. A small wind carries some of the spray against your face. Below the falls, the water runs over and around hundreds of boulders. You walk closer to the falls, leaping from boulder to boulder, and noticing that the water swirling around these rocks are teeming with small minnows and mer-folk, both adults and children.

At last, you see a flat rock along one side of the pool below the falls. You make your way over the boulders until you reach the ledge. You sit on this chair-like rock, your feet dangling over the edge, and watch the beauty of this waterfall. You hear within its roar a faint sound of singing and laughter. Taking a natural holey stone from your pocket, you hold it to the center of your forehead, between and just above your eyes. An amazing sight opens to you. Human-looking mer-folk are playing in the waterfall.

As you look down into the pools at the base of the falls, you see the children with their fish tails and upper human body. As they mature, these children will lose their tails and emerge on the slippery rocks as fully human-shaped beings.

As you look up at the falling water again, you see the iridescent sparkle of the scales as the adult mer-folk not only slide down the falls, but launch straight up the falling water, twisting and leaping. They are human-sized, with long, greenish-tinted hair. You are amazed at the acrobatic movements these beings can make as they ride the waterfall up and down. The laughter and singing you heard within the noise of the falls is coming from these happy water people.

As you sit on the rock chair, smiling at the mer-folk and their activities, a merman swims through the pool at the base of the falls toward your position. When he reaches you, he leaps straight out of the water to stand on the ledge beside you. Then he mimics you by sitting on the ledge and dangling his feet over the side.

"Why are you here, human?" the merman asks.

"Because I am studying Water magick," you answer and hold up your wrist encircled by the special bracelet.

"We work only with Water magick for healing," the merman says.

You look down and notice that the tiny scales that cover his entire body are arranged in various patterns, much as some fish have scale markings. When you meet his eyes, you see they are such a pale shade of bluish-gray that they seem almost without color. Pale green eyelashes match his long, greenish-tinted hair. You become aware that the merman is scrutinizing you as much as you are him.

"Will you teach me Water healing magick?" you ask.

The merman looks at you with his pale, cold eyes. "It is rare for a human to come to us." He nods his head yes. He talks to you about the importance of a balanced diet and how what and how much you eat can affect the development or diminishment of your psychic powers. Then he emphasizes the importance of drinking enough water each day to keep your internal system cleansed and healed.

He pauses a moment before revealing to you special Water healing magick, known only to the mer-folk. He also teaches you a chant to empower water to heal:

*Gentle as a drop of rain, stronger than the highest tide,*
*Filled with healing you shall be, and by my will shall*
*you abide.*

You open your stone pouch, and pour the tiny crystal points into the merman's hand in thanks for his teaching. When he smiles at you, you notice his sharp teeth for eating raw fish. He leaps back into the water and disappears under the waterfall.

You stand up on the ledge, watching the leaping, twisting mer-folk one last time. Then you think of your physical body. You slide down the tunnel of light into that body. You open your eyes. The meditation is finished.

## Lake Maidens Meditation

Visualize yourself standing on the shores of a large, deep lake, surrounded by beautiful forests. A full moon hangs over the lake, causing a single line of light to lead from the shoreline at your feet to the middle of the lake. Suddenly, a woman comes straight out of the lake and walks calmly down the line of moonlight toward you. You realize that she is the lady of this lake. You take a step backward so that she can walk directly onto the shore from the line of light. She is dressed in a medieval gown with long, flowing sleeves. A ring of keys hangs on her colorful belt. Her long, dark hair flows down her back to her waist, while her hands and wrists are covered with silver scales as if she wore special gloves. Hanging on a silver chain about her neck is a natural stone that is equally clear crystal and solid black. The stone glows, even though the moonlight does not touch it.

"Do you truly wish to see into your past lives and discover what you are to learn in this one?" the lady asks. "Past lives are most often sad, mundane things in which you were learning such virtues as patience, understanding, unconditional love, or control of temper. It is rare that humans lived lives of great importance."

When you answer yes, the lady takes you by the hand and leads you down the line of moonlight. At first, you fear that you will sink into the dark waters, but the lady reassures you that you are completely safe with her. When you reach the center of the lake, and the end of the line of moonlight, you find yourself walking down a flight of stairs into the dark water.

You emerge into a bright, colorful medieval hall. Banners and flags hang from the walls. The high, narrow windows appear to send bright light into the hall, even though it is night outside and the lake waters are black with the darkness. A long table is set near a fireplace. On it is a silver goblet set with colorful precious stones.

"Drink this," the lady says, as she hands you the goblet. "You will need the strength and willingness to see only truth in the ordeals before you."

You quickly drink the potion and set the goblet back on the table.

The lady leads the way down the hall to a tall, narrow door that has crystal patterns set directly into the wood. Taking the ring of keys from her belt, the lady chooses one and unlocks the door. As she pulls it open by its broad, iron handle, she motions for you to enter the hallway now visible before you.

You notice the stone-flagged floor is so clean that it shines in places. As you begin walking down this hall, you see what looks like windows on each side of the hallway. They are all dark, like the lake waters outside. Then, the next one is bright with a scene of people in another time.

"This is one of your past lives," the lady says softly. "It is connected to your present life in some way. Watch carefully."

You intuitively know that some of the people in the scene are in your present life, even though they do not look the same. You watch the action and listen to what is being said, until you realize what the connection is and whether or not you learn your lesson of that life.

You continue down the hallway with the lady, stopping to view three other lighted scenes of past lives. You are now at the end of the hallway, facing what appears to be a very large window, one that covers the entire wall.

"Are you now prepared to look at your present life to see how the past lives affect this one?" the lady asks.

When you answer yes, the lady takes her strange black and crystal pendant and touches it to the edge of the dark window. Instantly, the window comes alive with a moving scene from your present life. This scene may be of something going on in the present, or may come from the future.

"Do you understand how your past lives affect the present one? Do you understand what lesson you are to learn this time?" The lady watches you closely as you think about the past lives and the one you are living now.

Slowly, your intuition makes the connection, the lesson to be learned, the interaction of people over many lifetimes, the people you have positively or negatively touched each time, the opportunities you let pass you by because you feared change. You feel regret for some actions, satisfaction for others. You finally understand that it is the small things in life that are the powerful lessons: truth, kindness, patience, tolerance, helping others, just living your life the best you can at any given moment. One of the lessons of this lifetime is now revealed to you.

"That is enough for now," the lady says, again touching the window with her pendant. The scene fades to darkness.

The two of you go back up the hallway, through the open door, and into the bright medieval hall.

"Lady," you ask, "will you send me opportunities to gain my greatest personal desire?"

"I will help you by placing opportunities within your grasp, but you must seize them and work for that desire. It will not be given to you without effort." She touches the pendant to the spot over your heart. "May your future be filled with happiness and only a little sadness. May your karma be light and your destiny filled with love and excitement."

You know it is time to leave, so you think of your physical body. You slide down the tunnel of light into that body. You open your eyes. The meditation is finished.

# The Sea Sorcerer Meditation

Visualize yourself standing on the beach at night. A bright, full moon hangs overhead, its soft line rippling on the ocean surface as the waves come in to touch your feet. Across the open sea before you, you see a spot of white and hear the deep tones of a conch shell horn and the neighing of horses.

Swiftly, the Tritons blowing their horns rush to the shore. They are followed closely by the white pearly sea chariot of Poseidon, pulled by four horse-like hippocampus. The ancient sea god looks at you and points with his trident.

"Come. The sea sorcerer awaits you." Poseidon motions for you to enter the chariot with him.

You quickly climb into the chariot, marveling at the smoothness of the shell sides and the power you feel emanating from Poseidon. The sea god quickly turns his chariot to follow the blaring Tritons back out to sea. You grip the chariot side tightly as the sea-horses race across the dark ocean, the wind of their passage blowing back your hair. On and on Poseidon races until you see a tall, rather conical island jutting from the dark water. A carved path of steps winds around the rock isle to the top, from a narrow strip of beach at the bottom.

Poseidon turns the chariot sharply and brings it to a halt so that you can step onto the little beach. You thank the sea god for bringing you here. He nods his head and slaps the reins against the backs of the sea-horses. The chariot is quickly gone.

You pause to look at a light now glowing at the top of the island, then look at the long, steep flight of stairs. By now you understand that visualization can put you in any place or time. You visualize yourself at the top of the rocky island, where a lantern is hung beside a narrow door that leads to the inside of the peak.

You open the door and peer inside at the stairs leading downward, a light shining somewhere below.

"Come inside," a deep voice calls. "It is my time to test you. If you cannot pass my tests, you cannot be called an apprentice in Water magick."

You walk down the twisting stairs until you come to a room, the walls of which are covered with shelves full of books, scrolls, and ancient manuscripts. Near the far wall, you notice a faintly lighted break that is a continuation of the stairs. But your attention is centered on the sea sorcerer who sits at a candlelit table in the center of the room. The sorcerer is neither young nor old. He is dressed in a dark blue, open robe, the edges of which are marked with bright embroidery. Beneath the robe, he wears a white shirt, greenish-blue trousers, and black boots. His long, dark brown hair hangs to his shoulders.

You cannot decide if he is a member of the mer-folk or a human. He has no scales that you can see, or sharp teeth for eating raw fish. His skin coloring is not pale, and his eyes are not clear, pale gray, or watery blue. They are dark.

"Come," he says as he motions with one hand for you to follow. "We have no time to waste this night."

As he waved his hand, you knew the truth, for you saw the webs between his fingers. He is the child of a mermaid and a human male. You wonder how he came to live inside this towering rock, and why he is so powerful that it is the passing of his tests that gives you the opportunity to become a Water magick apprentice.

You follow the sorcerer down the next flight of stairs to another room. This room holds a circular table in the center with various types of seashells and a collection of glass floats on shelves near the walls. On the table are several items you recognize from your studies to this point.

"Tell me what each is and what it is used for." The sorcerer crosses his arms and watches quietly as you walk to the table. (Please note that some of the materials mentioned in this meditation and their magickal uses are described in-depth in Chapter 15.)

The first item you see is a long screw shell. You tell him what it is, and add, "This can be used as a wand."

You test a bowl of water with your fingers. You can feel the touch of the sea in it. You tell the sorcerer this. The next bowl is of springwater.

"These are cowrie shells, to be used in spells for prosperity," you say as you continue around the table. "This purple candle breaks bad luck, while this piece of amber will strengthen the spell and attract money. This red lump is dragon's blood, which also breaks curses. This is a bay leaf, which protects and stops interference from others."

"What spell can all these things be used in?" the sorcerer asks, his dark eyes looking straight into yours.

"A spell that would change your luck from bad to good. It would also break any curses sent at you and attract prosperity back into your life," you answer.

"Very good," the sea sorcerer says. "Follow me for the next test."

He leads the way down another set of stairs to yet another room. In this room is a small table, holding two closed boxes.

"Do not touch these," the sea sorcerer warns. "Hold your dominant hand over each box and tell me which one gives off positive or negative energy."

Carefully, you hold your dominant hand over each box and tell him which feels negative and which positive. The sorcerer gives a nod, and leads you down another flight of stairs to a darkened room lit only by candles in sconces hung on the walls. A high-backed chair sits in the center of the room, facing a thick cushion on the floor.

"Kneel here." The sea sorcerer points to the pillow as he sits in the chair. "Do you know why you are kneeling instead of sitting?" he asks.

"To learn humility and not think myself more powerful or knowledgeable than I am. And because this is part of the ceremony to become an apprentice," you say.

The sea sorcerer laughs and nods his head. "Very apt and very clever, Apprentice." He picks up a long wand tipped with a merkabah crystal that is leaning against his chair. "Remember, you are in the tadpole stage of learning about Water magick. It takes much study, practice, and patience to raise yourself step by step to the next level of magick. No one ever becomes a Master, because no one can know all there is to learn about the magick of the mer-folk and Water."

He taps you lightly on each side of your head with the wand. Laying it aside, he stands and hangs a special symbol around your neck. This may be a stone, a shell, or a metal pendant of some kind. This will appear to you sometime in life, and you will have the opportunity to obtain it in physical form.

"Now, Apprentice, you may leave." The sea sorcerer gestures toward the stairs, a slight smile curving his mouth.

You shake your head no, for you know there is an easier way. Then you think of your physical body. You slide down the tunnel of light into your body, the sorcerer's laugh echoing behind you. You open your eyes. The meditation is finished.

## Exploring Under the Sea Meditation

Visualize yourself walking down the sunny beach toward the ocean. You touch the crystal you are wearing around your neck. You can just see a merman waiting for you near some rocks, the sun glinting off the metal tips of his trident. You will yourself to be with him, and you are there in the water beside him.

"Would you like to explore the warm waters of the tropical seas?" he asks with a smile. "There are many different things to see there."

As soon as you answer yes, instantly you and the merman are swimming underwater in the warm waters of the Caribbean. You do not know the names of the islands you pass. You are far more interested in the amazing things you see in the water and on the ocean floor.

The merman guides you to an area where great blocks of smoothed stones run like a wide avenue deep into the sea. You swim along, following this ancient stone roadway, the merman watching carefully for sharks. Soon, no sun can filter through the ocean depths. Your crystal begins to glow with a brilliant light that illuminates everything around for many feet.

At last you come to the remains of a great city, so deep in the ocean that no human has ever looked upon it before. You do not recognize the letters and symbols carved into the stone blocks of what looks like an ancient temple. As you pass the open doorway to this temple, your crystal is pulled straight out on its chain as if attracted to a powerful magnet. It glows brighter, and there is an answering light coming from inside the temple. You feel charges of powerful energy filling your crystal pendant. As you start to enter the building, the merman grabs your arm and shakes his head no.

"It is not safe to enter there," he says telepathically. "This is part of the last pieces of Atlantis to sink into the ocean. Even our elders do not come here. They say we may swim through and look, but are not to enter any of the buildings. There are powerful things here we do not understand."

Regretfully, you swim away with him. You rise higher in the ocean so that the sunlight now glows through the water. You take notice of the brightly colored schools of different fish that swim back and forth around you. There are many varieties of sea animals and plants along your route. As you near the land, where the ocean is not as deep, you see several stingrays lying on the sand below you.

The merman motions with his trident for you to follow him. You are surprised to find that you can feel the different currents of the ocean against your skin. It is like learning to feel the currents in the air when you are weather-working.

Soon, the merman points downward with his trident. You look and see the shattered remains of a sunken ship. As you swim closer, a shark suddenly glides out of the wreck, its tiny cold eyes fixed on you. The merman sings a sharply discordant note and threatens with his trident. The shark quickly swims away.

The two of you float into the small, open part left of the ship. There you see broken, encrusted lanterns and metal dishes. Outside again, you scan the ocean floor until you see the faint glint of gold half buried in the sand. You scoop away the sand to uncover a mass of Spanish doubloons, encrusted together. You drop the doubloons back where they were. It would require special care to remove any of these treasures from the sea.

As you move along the coast, following a current of strong water, the merman points out rusty remains of other ships and airplanes, all sunk or dumped into the ocean. Even the water begins to look and feel foul. The two of you move farther away from the land into clearer water. Soon, you are near the Caribbean Islands again.

You slowly drift along as you watch the various fishes and sea creatures going about their daily lives. You think of the wonders of the ocean, and wish that everyone could see them. But you know too many people would want to destroy rather than just look and admire.

Both you and the merman look toward the surface at the same time. You can feel the prickle of a coming storm against your skin. You notice that even the fish feel the change and act differently. You realize how much you have changed since you started your work with mer-folk and Water magick. You realize that the sky, the earth, and the sea are closely connected, all responding to what happens to one of them. Your feelings of connections keep spreading out until you at last grasp the idea that "all are one"—that everything in the universe, including you, is connected to everything else.

As the merman and you swim swiftly away from the storm area, he looks at you and smiles. "You are learning, Apprentice," he says with his thoughts. "Add this to your lesson for today: All things on this plane are connected also with everything in the Otherworld plane. None of us are separate."

Soon you recognize the feel of your "home" water. You smile at the merman and nod your thanks as you swim back to the beach. It has been an entertaining and adventuresome day.

Then you think of your physical body. You slide down the tunnel of light into that body. You open your eyes. The meditation is finished.

# CHAPTER 15

# Mermaid and Water Spells

Learning to meditate and visualize is very important to the successful completion of spells. Visualization uses astral energy to build your desired results on the astral plane before they are manifest on the physical plane. Without visualization, you can't expect your spells to turn out as you wish.

The lists in the first part of this chapter are basic to all magickal spells. They have been placed here together so the magician has access to everything needful in one place. She or he can quickly decide on any substitutions they wish to make for items used in a certain spell, or conveniently select components when they create a spell of their own.

When working Water spells, of course, the magician must always have charged water on hand. It is also useful to have beach sand, pebbles, and small pieces of driftwood available, as these add to the spell's power and connection with the mer-folk.

If you use starfish or little seahorses, please buy them already dried to be sold. It is also possible to purchase baskets of various types of seashells, as well as glass floats, if you wish to use them in spellworking.

Basic tools you may need include: metal candleholders, small bowl for water, small metal bowl or cauldron for paper burning and herb burning, incense holder or can of sand, small bowl for sand, small pieces of paper and a pen, tray or special altar for indoor rituals.

Please think carefully before you do any spellwork in which you specifically name a person, such as in love and divorce. Naming a specific person is interfering with free will and trying to control him or her. Sooner or later, karma will make you pay for this. It is much safer, for example, to ask for your perfect mate to appear or for the unhappy couple's problem to be solved in a positive way.

Clean up carefully after each ritual. Dispose of any remaining candle wax and paper ashes in the garbage. Herbs may safely be sprinkled on the ground if they were not burned.

## Candles

It is best if you use small votive or birthday candles for spellwork. These burn out quickly, however, and the birthday candles may be difficult to find in certain colors. If you have a spell that needs a great amount of power behind it, do your spell indoors and use a votive or a seven-day candle (which comes in its own tall glass container).

When preparing to burn a votive candle, hold on to the top of the wick and remove the metal tab from the bottom, then place the candle in a heavy metal bowl to burn. If you coat the bottom of the bowl or cauldron generously with the appropriate essential oil, it will be much easier to clean out any remaining wax later.

# Basic Color Correspondences

Black: Absorbs and removes any negative vibrations or events; reverses, uncrosses, and binds negative forces; releases and breaks up blockages and stagnant situations; protects.

Blue: Use light blue for wisdom, truth, good health, happiness, harmony in relationships, and inner peace. Use royal blue for loyalty, group success, and expanding psychic powers.

Brown: Attracts money and financial success because of its ability to influence the Earth Elementals. Also helpful for concentration, intuition, grounding and centering your energies, and communicating with nature spirits.

Gold or very clear light yellow: If circumstances are out of your control, this color can attract fast luck. Useful for divination, intuition, money, healing, and happiness.

Green: Long connected with abundance, fertility, wealth, success, marriage, communication with nature spirits, and bringing balance to an unstable situation.

Indigo: This dark purplish-blue color balances out karma and neutralizes any magick coming from another person. Also useful in stopping gossip and lies.

Magenta: This hue of candle is burned with other candles because of its tendency to make things happen faster. It can be burned alone for exorcism.

Orange: A very powerful color, burn this to change your luck and attract good things into your life. Also used to draw creativity, success, energy, attraction, and mental agility.

Pink: Although this color can banish depression and hatred, it also attracts pure love, friendship, romance, and spiritual awakening.

Purple: The energy of this very powerful color is difficult to handle. It helps with court cases, business success, removing jinxes and curses, breaking bad luck, contacting spirit, spiritual protection, wisdom, and gaining higher psychic abilities.

Red: Attracts strength, energy, physical desire, passionate love, courage, and protects against psychic attack.

Silver or very clear light gray: Helps remove negative powers, neutralizes any troublesome situation, and repels destructive forces.

White: Because white is a highly balanced spiritual color, use it whenever in doubt about a candle color. It is also useful in contacting spiritual guides and helpers, balancing your aura, growing spiritually, and destroying negative energies.

Yellow: Attracts greater mind powers, knowledge, creativity, concentration, imagination, knowledge of medicine, and healing.

# Herbs

If you burn herbs, you will need religious charcoal blocks, placed in a heavy metal bowl or cauldron. These religious blocks ignite quickly, as they are permeated with a substance that makes lighting easy. You may wish to break them in half and use only half a block at a time.

## Herb Correspondences

Basil: Exorcise negativity from an area or building.

Bay laurel: Protects and stops interference.

Chamomile: Used to get a marriage proposal and bring luck in gambling.

Clove: Used to gain a desire or banish evil.

Dragon's blood: Attracts good luck and love; banishes curses.

Frankincense: Purification, exorcism, protection.

Ginger: Love, success, prosperity.

Jasmine: Attracts love and strengthens psychic abilities.

Lavender: Draws love, money, and helpful spirits.

Lemon verbena: Repels unwanted lovers.

Marjoram: Protection.

Myrrh: Purification and protection.

Patchouli: Will break any spell. Aids in bringing back a lost love and defeating enemies.

Peppermint: Purification. Attracts love and increases psychic ability.

Pine: Purification, protection.

Rose petals: Creates love; brings happiness to a home.

Rosemary: Helps in healing and exorcisms.

Sage: Purification, wisdom, protection.

Sandalwood: Used for protection and exorcism.

Thyme: Cleanses the aura and stops nightmares.

Vervain: Repels psychic attack; also helps in gaining love and wealth.

Yarrow: Used for divination and love spells.

# Incense

It is easiest to burn incense sticks, especially the shorter ones, by sticking them upright in a small can of sand. However, you may use a holder for incense sticks or set the cone directly on the sand.

## Incense Correspondences

Balance: Jasmine, orange, rose.

Banishing and release: Cedar, clove, patchouli, rue, vervain.

Binding: Cypress, dragon's blood, pine.

Blessing: Carnation, frankincense, lotus.

Changes: Dragon's blood, peppermint.

Contacting the astral plane: Frankincense.

Creativity: Honeysuckle, lilac, lotus, rose, vervain.

Determination, courage: Allspice, dragon's blood, musk, rosemary.

Divination: Acacia, cinnamon, honeysuckle, lilac, rose, thyme.

Energy, power: Bay, carnation, cinnamon, dragon's blood, frankincense, ginger, musk, pine, rosemary.

Exorcism: Basil, bay, cedar, frankincense, myrrh, pine, rosemary, vervain.

Good luck, justice: Bayberry, cedar, cinnamon, honeysuckle, jasmine, lotus, strawberry, violet.

Happiness, harmony: Basil, cedar, clove, fir, gardenia, jasmine, lavender, lilac, myrrh, patchouli, rose, ylang-ylang.

Healing: Carnation, cedar, cinnamon, clove, gardenia, lavender, lotus, orange, rosemary, sandalwood.

Inspiration and wisdom: Bay, clove, fir, rosemary, sage.

Love: Amber, frangipani, gardenia, honeysuckle, jasmine, lavender, musk, rose, strawberry, vanilla, violet, ylang-ylang.

Money and prosperity: Bayberry, bergamot, cinnamon, honeysuckle, jasmine.

Protection, defense: Bay, cypress, dragon's blood, fir, frankincense, juniper, lotus, patchouli, pine, rosemary, sandalwood.

Psychic abilities, strengthening: Honeysuckle, lemon, lotus, mimosa, wisteria.

Purification: Bay, cedar, cinnamon, dragon's blood, frankincense, lavender, marjoram, myrrh, peppermint, rosemary, sage.

Remove a curse or hex: Cedar, myrrh, vetiver.

Spirituality: Frankincense, lotus, myrrh, sandalwood.

Success: Ginger.

Willpower: Rosemary.

# Oils

Oils have been an important ingredient in magickal spells and religious ceremonies for thousands of years. Oils are never to be swallowed or taken internally, as this can be dangerous. As well, direct contact with some oils may irritate the skin and can be dangerous if you are pregnant, nursing, or suffer from some medical conditions. Their primary uses are to scent talisman bags, incense sticks, or to rub on the outside of candles during specific rituals. Some oils, such as pure jasmine, are extremely expensive; in such cases, I have found that the artificial forms may be used.

**Oil Correspondences**

Bayberry: Prosperity, gaining control of a situation.

Bergamot: Money, happiness.

Carnation: Healing, strength.

Cedar: Purification, removing curses.

Cinnamon: Money, energy, purification.

Clove: Healing, creativity.

Dragon's blood: Purification, protection, exorcism, removes hexes and curses.

Frangipani: Useful in attracting the perfect mate; love.

Frankincense and myrrh: Purification, protection, healing.

(Either oil used alone will achieve the same results, but equal parts mixed together are more powerful.)

Gardenia: Love, healing, happiness.

Honeysuckle: Attracts money and strengthens psychic abilities.

Jasmine: Love, money.

Lavender: Healing, love.

Lotus: Purification, protection.

Musk: Attracts the opposite sex; prosperity.

Patchouli: Love, protection, purification.

Peppermint: Creativity, money.

Pine: Cleansing, protection.

Rose: Love, cleansing.

Rosemary: Protection.

Sage: Purification, finding wisdom.

Sandalwood: Cleansing.

Vanilla: Attracts sexual love and aids mental powers.

Violet: Love, good luck, finding a solution.

Ylang-ylang: Love, harmony.

# Shells

All shells in general hold the power of the seas, which is one of the most powerful of natural forces. Therefore, any type of shell used in a spell makes it stronger. The following list of shells are ones that are easily found in shops and can be purchased. However, it is not necessary that you purchase one of each, or any at all. You can use whatever shells you find washed up on the beach or baskets of shells you find in gift and hobby shops. (I have added short notes to the shells that have a certain history attached to them.)

## Types of Shells and Some Uses

Abalone: Sacred to the Native Americans, this shell can be filled with a layer of sand to protect it when burning herbs and papers.

Augur shell: This shell and the screw shell look like miniature unicorn horns. If you can find a long one, it can be used as a wand.

Boat ear moon shell.

Clam shell: Use for love and passionate love spells.

Conch: Otherworld messages from your teachers and guides can be heard when this shell is held to the ear. (Types of conch include Pacific crown, spider, and West Indian crown.)

Cowrie: This little shell has been a Goddess shell for thousands of years. It represents the female in general, as well as female-type energy and prosperity. The tiger cowrie is one specific kind.

Dove shell, common.

Frog shell, California and spiny.

Limpet.

Oyster shell.

Sand dollar.

Scallop shell.

Screw shell.

Sea mussel shell.

Triton, Oregon and trumpet.

Winkle.


## Stones

If you cannot find these stones in either a tumbled or an unfinished state, you may use jewelry into which particular stones are set.

## Stone Correspondences

Agate: Grounds, strengthens the mind and body, brings out the truth, and protects against all dangers, especially black magick.

Agate, eye: Protection; turns away curses.

Agate, fire: Increases personal power and the ability to operate efficiently.

Agate, moss: Attracts good health and long life, protects the aura, and helps in opening the third eye.

Amber: Heals, soothes, increases the strength of spells, and attracts money.

Amethyst: Cuts through illusion, increases psychic abilities, attracts good fortune and creativity, and ensures justice in court.

Aventurine: Repels anxiety and fears, attracts good luck and creativity.

Beryl: A stone of slow-acting energy, it is useful for keeping others from draining off your energy.

Bloodstone: Attracts long life, prosperity, success, and good health; guards against deception and cheats.

Carnelian: Fast-acting, this stone can speed up manifestations; realigns all the bodies: physical, mental, emotional, and spiritual.

Chalcedony: Repels illusions, overcomes evil, and brings good fortune.

Chrysocolla: Helps in releasing old resentments and guilt; can help form a bridge between the physical and astral planes.

Citrine: Strengthens self-esteem, protects the aura, helps to deal with difficult karma.

Emerald: Helps with dreams and meditation; attracts prosperity, peace, balance, love, and healing.

Fluorite: heals all the chakras, cleanses the aura, and is excellent for connecting with the Akashic Records for answers to your past lives.

Fossils: Helps with protection and looking into your past lives.

Garnet: Increases productivity and helps you to stay focused.

Geodes: Extremely useful for past-life meditations.

Hematite: Reduces stress and helps get a favorable outcome in court.

Holey stones: Look through the hole in the stone while in the moonlight to see mermaids, faeries, and other similar beings. Before starting meditation, hold a holey stone against your Third Eye to contact your teachers and guides.

Jade: Powerfully balances the emotions and dispels negativity.

Labradorite: Use to manifest results to improbable situations.

Lapis lazuli: Releases tension; balances and cleanses the chakras; helps to communicate with your spirit guides.

Lodestone: Helps to communicate with dolphins and whales; draws in good luck, love, and money.

Malachite: Repels evil spirits, black magick, and accidents; strengthens the intuition and understanding.

Marble: Helps to focus on spiritual needs and studies.

Merkabah crystal: The name of this man-made stone takes its name from the ancient Egyptian Mer (place of ascending), Ka (spirit), and Ba (light, vehicle of vehicles). This small crystal with eight protrusions is a controller of time-shifting and the intersection of light dimensions. Carry it with you after a spell to open your consciousness to other dimensions.

Moonstone: Relieves stress and tension and removes emotional blockages between lovers.

Obsidian, black: Helps you face challenges and past-life lessons.

Obsidian, snowflake: Aids in thinking clearly and logically.

Onyx, black: Will destroy negative energy sent by others; helps in feeling secure.

Pearl: Reveals the truth in any situation. (Man-made pearls may be used instead of real ones.)

Pyrite or fool's gold: Strengthens the will and eases anxiety.

Quartz crystal, clear: Balances emotions, heals, stimulates thinking, transmits and amplifies energy, and enhances communication with astral beings.

Quartz, rose: Use to attract a true companion or lover.

Quartz, smoky: Breaks up subconscious blockages and negativity, protects and helps with psychic work.

Rhodochrosite: Helps in finding a true love and/or soulmate, clears mental blockages, and heals emotional wounds.

Ruby: Removes all sense of limitation and attracts passionate love.

Sapphire: Stimulates psychic ability, helps to contact spirit guides, seals the aura, and intensifies spells.

Tiger's eye: Protects against all kinds of dark magick and aids in divination into past lives.

Topaz: Repels enchantments, aids with messages from the astral realm, prevents accidents, and repels envy.

Tourmaline: Protects as it strengthens self-assurance and inspires creativity.

Turquoise: Emotional balance, peace of mind, reconciliation between friends and lovers, prosperity; can build a "bridge" between worlds.

## Inviting the Presence of the Mer-Folk

It is always best to have the help of mer-folk guides and teachers whenever you work spells that have to do with Water magick. They can teach you through subconscious impressions what is right or wrong for you, as an individual Water magician, to do. Not every magician works the same way.

The same ritual applies whether you are at the beach; near a waterfall, river, or stream; or in a wetland or swampy area. You want to invite the mer-folk by leaving a gift but remain as inconspicuous as possible. If you find that another magician has already made a gifting spot, simply add a few of your gifts to the others rather than make a new place. That is, unless the gifting spot feels negative, which could happen but is unlikely.

Make a circular, shallow place in the sand or earth in a place that ordinary people are not apt to go. Thinly line this gifting place with a layer of sea grass or whatever grass grows nearby.

Into this "nest," place your gifts of tiny shells, sea pebbles, a pinch of ground sage, and a small piece each of rough or tumbled agate and black onyx. Lightly sprinkle sea salt over the gift offering. Hold both hands over the offering, and chant:

*Mer-folk in this place and time,*
*Hear me chant this little rhyme.*
*Come as helpers, teachers bold,*
*Guides to knowledge true and old.*
*Make my magick strong and true,*
*And for this help I do thank you.*

Walk away and do not look back at your gift. Gifts to the mer-folk must be freely given without any expectations in return. This is when the mer-folk will help you in your Water magick—not when you have strings attached.

# Making Friends With Friendly, Fabulous Sea Creatures

First consult Chapter 4 to make certain you know which sea creatures, natural or astral, are friendly toward humans. Then review Chapter 12 on the dangerous water creatures, so you can avoid calling up their negative vibrations.

Set up your tray or altar with one small bowl of sand, one of charged water, and a little sea salt on a saucer. Put a pinch each of dragon's blood, lavender, and sage on the saucer beside the salt. Prepare a light-blue votive candle in a metal bowl or cauldron with a little lotus oil in the bottom to keep the wax from sticking. If you have a particular animal or animals that you would like to contact and work with, place pictures of them on the altar or tray. If you cannot find pictures, clearly write each name on a piece of paper and place those on the altar.

Hold your hands over the altar and chant:

*All the creatures of the sea*
*That I have named here, come to me,*
*To teach me what I need to know*
*To make our budding friendship grow.*
*Water, sand, and herbs of grace*
*Are lit by a candle in this place. (Light the votive candle.)*
*These are my gifts, you of the sea.*
*Magick is my will. So shall it be.*

Meditate on each sea creature until you can see it clearly in your mind. Then thank them all for their presence. Leave the candle to burn out.

For the following spells, you will want to have a large tray or your altar ready to use. (The tray is for those who do not have an altar and may need to carefully move their spell material to a different room.)

Any wax left from burned candles should be put into the garbage as soon as it is cool enough. Any energy put into the candles will be gone by the time they are completely burned.

## Banishing Spell No 1

Banishing spells are usually done to permanently remove someone from your life or to remove negative thoughts and vibrations sent by another person. Most of the trouble that makes your life uncomfortable is called by ill-wishing, or jealous thoughts of other people.

Carefully wash a piece of tumbled obsidian or black onyx in charged water. Dry it completely. Put a thin layer of sea salt in a small bowl, and lay the stone on top of the salt. Chant:

*All harmful thoughts and negative people, leave my life.*
*Only happiness and good things come to me.*
*Blessed water, purify me and this stone.*
*So from ill-wishing I am now free.*

Touch the center of your forehead, the palm of each hand, and the top of each foot with charged water. Wait for twenty-four hours, then you can carry the stone with you each day or leave it in a central position somewhere in your home.

# Banishing Spell Nº2

This is a good spell to use when the vibrations in your home do not feel positive, when you have had negative visitors, or when there is strife within the household. It can be repeated for five consecutive days after the new moon, if you feel it is necessary.

On the new moon, grind one teaspoon of dried basil with three teaspoons of sea salt. Make certain the mixture is ground very fine. Pour into a small bowl and set it on a layer of sand decorated with seashells and other things to remind you of the powerful sea and Water magick. Leave it there while you chant three times:

> *Magick of water, hear my call.*
> *Powerful sea, help cleanse all.*
> *Destroy the bad, create only good*
> *So that this house feels as it should.*

Moving in a clockwise direction in each room, sprinkle a tiny bit of the mixture in each corner, while saying:

> *All negative out. Only good remains.*

Include all closets, too. When finished, light a white candle and patchouli incense. Let the candle burn for one hour before extinguishing it.

# Better Business Spell Nº1

Sometimes your business goes into a slump that you just can't understand. The first thing you should do is a banishing spell. (Your establishment may be plagued by negative thoughts sent by jealous people.) If it is a bad time of year for sales or you simply need to draw more customers, then a better business spell is useful.

Start by carrying a burning frankincense incense stick through the entire store. Follow this by sprinkling charged water into every corner. At your desk or the place where you do your financial work, fill a tiny vial with sand, cap it, and set it where you can see it whenever you work. Do the same with a vial of charged water with a little sea salt in it.

Each morning, before you open your business, stand near your work space and chant softly:

*Ancient mer-folk, wise and bold,*
*Bring me money I can hold.*
*Customers and opportunity,*
*Fill my business with serenity.*
*Cleanse all negativity*
*With the mystic power of the sea.*

## Better Business Spell № 2

If your business is within your home, or you work primarily from your home, the first thing you need to do is a house cleansing. Grind a teaspoon each of dried basil and lavender with two teaspoons of sea salt. Pour this mixture into a small bowl. Hold your hands over it and chant:

*I pour into you the power of sea and Water,*
*That only prosperity is washed my way.*

Cut out two squares of green cloth, about two inches wide. Put the right sides together and stitch a seam around three sides. Turn it right side out. Put three small cowrie shells into the bag along with at least half of the herb and salt mixture. Sew the top of the bag closed. This good-luck-for-business bag can be carried with you at all times.

Put the remaining herb and salt mixture into a container. Each day, sprinkle a very small amount in your mailbox and across the threshold of your main business door. This will attract the business prosperity you need.

## Change Your Luck Spell

If your life seems to be stuck in a negative mode, or you just can't get out of a rut that is bringing you nothing but misery, it is time to do a spell for changing your luck. On your tray or altar, set two small bowls of sand. In one, place a piece of religious charcoal block and light it. It will sizzle and flash around the edges until it is lit. Prepare a purple or orange votive candle and set it in the second bowl of sand. Light the candle.

Visualize the ferocious sea-lions, those astral lions of the sea that come and go between this world and the Otherworld. When you can see the sea-lion in your mind, visualize three of them together, and know that they are ready, awaiting your call.

If you wish, you can burn a magenta candle in another bowl to speed up the manifestation of your desire.

Drop a pinch of dragon's blood powder onto the charcoal block and say:

*My life is purified of all harmful influences.*
*Nothing and no one can affect my luck again.*

Put another pinch of dragon's blood on the burning block, then hold your dominant hand near one side of the candle, saying:

*My luck has changed from bad to good.*
*Sea-lions, go forth to aid this spell,*
*The power of Water magick changes all,*
*As does the blessed water from holy wells.*
*I turn from the bad and grasp tight the new.*
*Mer-folk who help, I do thank you.*

Visualize the three sea-lions pouncing on a black ball, ripping and tearing, until only a shining ball of clear light is left. Thank them for helping you uncover your good luck. Add more incense and leave the candles to burn out.

## Cleansing Spell

Sometimes, such as when you purchase something from a secondhand store or have had visitors who touch things all over your house, you need to remove negative vibrations. The spell for cleansing a business will also work for cleansing your house, in general. However, a purchased object that has negative vibrations requires a different procedure.

First, you must determine if it is safe to wash the object in either salt water or cold, running water. Be aware that some statues and other items are made of materials that are damaged by water. If it will not be damaged by water, wash it carefully in sea water, followed by a rinse in cold, running water. When you are drying the object, say:

*Of all ill you are free.*
*As my will so shall it be.*

If the object cannot be submerged or sprinkled with water, you will need to use another method. Put a thin layer of sand in a large enough bowl or tray, with a layer of sea salt on top of the sand. Set the object on the salt and sand. Leave it there for five days. At the end of that time, before you remove the object, chant:

*Cleansed by salt and by sand,*
*You Come pure into my hand.*

## Court Case Spell

The night before you go to court, burn a purple candle and frankincense incense on your tray or altar. On a small piece of paper, draw a sketch of Poseidon's three-pronged trident. Leave the paper on the altar overnight. Let the candle burn out.

The next morning as you prepare to go to court, either put the paper in your pocket or pin it to the inside of your bra. As you do this, chant:

*Mermaids, Poseidon, all of the sea,*
*Today, bring only justice to me.*

## Divination Spell

If possible, burn a gold candle and jasmine incense while you are doing a reading for yourself or for others. Set your merkabah crystal or a large pointed crystal between the candle and the incense. Hold the cards, runes, or whatever divination tool you will be using in both hands and say:

> Lady of the Lake, who sees both past and future, show
> only the truth to me.

Do your layout or casting. Give the reading as you are led by the Lady. However, if you see great misfortune or death, do not reveal this to the other person. Instead, simply warn them to take extra care for the next few months.

## Dream Spell

Often when you have a problem you can't solve, you will get an answer during your sleep at night. Just before you go to bed, whisper your problem into a conch or other spiral shell. Set the shell by your bed, and say:

> My mind is open to solutions,
> End of problems, resolutions.
> Bring me the key in sleep so sound
> That an answer comes, simple or profound.

## Gamblers' Spell and Charms

Carry several small cowrie shells along with your favorite good luck charm. They can just be loose in your pocket or placed in a pouch and then tucked into a pocket. Before you start your game of chance, silently say:

> Lady Luck, so beautiful and bright,
> Shine your favor on me here this night.

# Healing Spell

Have the sick person sit in a comfortable chair or lie down. If possible, have them hold a clear quartz crystal in each hand. Using your screw shell wand, and without touching the person, move the wand from the head to the feet on all sides. As you do this, visualize your movements followed by brilliant white light. When you are finished, hold the wand horizontally over the patient's abdomen and say:

*Water cleanses.*
*The sea cleanses.*
*The power of the mer-folk cleanses.*
*All disease is cast out, the body once more made whole.*

Put one drop of charged water on the center of the center of the person's forehead.

# Love Spell

When you do love spells, please do not use a specific name, which would be interfering with another's free will. Besides, that person may not be perfect for you and you will be stuck with someone unsuitable. Keep your thoughts centered on "the perfect man/woman for me." This leaves the field wide open for you to have many choices.

Have your tray or altar cleaned and ready. Burn jasmine incense. Place one red and one pink candle in small bowls of sand. Place pieces of pink quartz around a mermaid statue or picture in the center of the altar.

As you light the pink candle, say:

*True love comes to me. A soulmate, friend.*

As you light the red candle, say:

*One who will love me to the end.*

Close your eyes and visualize your mermaid coming to life and singing as she sits on rocks at the ocean. She is singing a beautiful love song that you feel penetrate your complete body. She is making a love magnet of you to attract the right love.

When she finishes, open your eyes and say as you look at the mermaid:

*I open my heart, my life, my hands,*
*To the one who will love me for who I am.*
*Let true love enter my heart,*
*So strong it will never part.*

## Marriage Spell

Humans, as well as the mer-folk, were not created to live alone. There is someone out there for everyone. We must be open-minded and prepared to take advantage of opportunities that come our way. Two people in love should give themselves time to know each other's habits and ways of doing things. It is also necessary to learn to communicate and compromise, for any marriage to work. This spell is not to get someone to marry you, but for a blessed marriage.

Prepare your tray or altar with two small bowls of sand. Put a pink candle in one and a green candle in the other. Burn jasmine incense. Set your merkabah crystal and several cowrie shells in the middle of the altar, beside a statue of a mermaid.

> *Mer-folk of the sea,*
> *Who know the blessings of life to be,*
> *Bless my marriage—make it strong.*
> *Keep us happy for many years long.*
> *May the two of us be one,*
> *Until our lives are done.*

## Divorce Spell

Sometimes, no matter what one does, a divorce becomes inevitable. You and your significant other may have grown apart instead of together. Perhaps one of you has broken vows or become abusive. Maybe one or both realize that you must part and would prefer to do so with the least amount of stress. A peaceful divorce is rare. However, an equitable divorce with neither side becoming hurt more is usually the best one can hope for.

Arrange your tray or altar with a small bowl of sand into which you place an indigo candle. Burn patchouli incense for the releasing of both the marriage and any negative feelings that arise from the divorce. Take a photo that shows just the two of you together. Cut off the side with you, and lay it on the altar. Roll up the side with your spouse and tie it with black thread. Put your wedding ring on top of your part of the photo. Say:

> *From this day forward I am free of your influence.*
> *I will create a new me and a new life, full of happiness.*

Burn your spouse's part of the photo in a metal bowl or cauldron. Say:

*I release you to find your happiness with another.*
*The tie we had between us is forever cut.*
*We each go our separate ways with no ill thoughts.*

Leave the candles to burn out. Flush the ashes of the photo down the toilet. If you wish to continue wearing your wedding ring, you may want to consider wearing it on the right hand now.

## Prosperity Spell

Arrange your tray or altar with two small bowls of sand. Put a dark-green candle in one and a brown candle in the other. Burn bayberry and honeysuckle incense. Have one large cowrie shell and several smaller ones on the side for use later. Take the largest denomination of paper money you have and lay it in the center of the altar. Light the candles and say:

*Prosperity, success, all come to me.*
*As is my will, so shall it be.*

Take the smaller cowrie shells and, as you place them in a circle around the paper money, say:

*I circle my financial life with success,*
*with thought, work, and preparedness.*
*The water folk and mermaids free*
*Will help me win prosperity.*

Lay the large cowrie shell on top of the paper money. Say:

*Large becomes larger.*
*My money attracts more money.*
*Opportunities to better myself become frequent.*
*I thank all the mer-folk and magickal water beings who*
    *help me.*

Leave the large cowrie shell on the money for at least twenty-four hours. Let the candles burn out. If you wish to speed the spell, burn a magenta candle between the green and brown candles.

## Protection Spell

Sometimes a simple banishing spell will not completely remove all of a problem. Then you must do a protection spell so you are not affected by people's ill-wishing or angry resentment, for whatever reason.

On your tray or altar, burn a stick each of pine and frank-incense incense together. Place a small bowl of sand on the left side with a red candle in it. Place another bowl on the right side with a silver candle in it.

Place a small hand mirror and a bowl of charged water in the center. Lay your screw shell wand beside the mirror.

As you light the red candle, say:

*I draw to myself all energy needed to protect myself and*
*my loved ones.*

As you light the silver candle, say:

*The power of the mermaids and all the water folk is with*
*me at all times.*

Sprinkle a few drops of charged water on the mirror's reflective surface and say:

*Like a powerful laser, this reflective mirror burns away*
*the influence of anyone or anything that would cause*
*harm to me and mine.*

With your wand in your dominant hand and the mirror in the other, face the north and say:

*Mer-folk, aid me in destroying all physical harm coming*
*from the north.*

Turn clockwise to the east, still holding up the wand and mirror, and say:

*Mer-folk, aid me in destroying all harmful thoughts com-*
*ing from the east.*

Turn to the south and say:

*Mer-folk, aid me in destroying all harmful spells and*
*curses coming from the south.*

Turn to the west and say:

*Mer-folk, aid me in destroying all harmful emotions com-*
*ing from the west.*

Stand before the altar as you put the wand and mirror back in the center of it and say:

*I ask only for protection, not revenge.*
*I ask for what is mine by right of life itself.*
*Build a strong web of Water magick about me and mine,*
*That all harmful things may not reach me.*

# Remove Hexes and Curses Spell

Sometimes, what seems to be a long streak of bad luck is more than that. Not many magicians will go so far as to lay a hex or curse on another person, but a few are unethical enough to do so. In such cases, you must protect yourself by breaking the curse. It usually only takes one determined try, and it is gone.

Arrange three small bowls of sand on your tray or altar in a triangular position. Place a purple candle in each one. Burn one stick of patchouli and one stick of frankincense incense, both excellent for exorcisms and the breaking of curses.

Arrange the roughest-looking seashells you have on your altar. The sharp points and rough surfaces cut up the curse-thoughts aimed at you. Light the purple at the top of the triangular shape. Say:

*I close forever the door between this evil magician and me.*

Light the purple candle on the left, and say:

*I cleanse all that has been touched by this evil spell.*

Light the purple candle on the right, and say:

*I send this curse and everything evil born from it into the earth where it is transmuted into positive energy.*

Face the altar with your arms raised. Say:

*The curse is broken.*
*I am set free.*
*As my will, so shall it be!*

Leave the candles to burn out.

# Travelers' Spell

For this spell you will need either a small, dried starfish and seahorse or metal images of these sea creatures. If you cannot find metal charms in these particular shapes, find charms of mermaids and other sea life. If you use charms, hang them on a chain you can wear while you travel.

Prepare your tray or altar by placing seashells on it. Put an orange candle in a small bowl of sand, and place the bowl in the center and toward the back of the altar. Using your index finger, coat the top of the candle with either pine or rosemary oil. Light the candle and burn the sandalwood incense.

Move your travel charms back and forth over both the incense smoke and candle heat, saying:

*As your true images travel in the great sea, so must I
journey from one place to another. Fill these tokens with
the strongest of Water magick that I may be fully protected.*

Do this cleansing and chanting three times before you put on the chain holding the charms. If you have the small, dried versions, put them into a tiny pouch you can carry in your pocket or pin to the inside of your bra.

Remember to thank your magickal mermaids and other helpers when you return from your journey.

# Unblocking Spell

Blockages are caused by old programming in the subconscious mind. Even if another person appears to be at fault, they only block you because you are reacting to their behavior in a programmed manner. Subconscious programming is forever in that part of your mind. The only way to handle it is to recognize the programming at once and refuse to react to it.

Arrange your tray or altar with a small bowl of sand at each back corner. Place a black candle in each bowl. Between these candles, burn frankincense or patchouli incense. In the center of the altar, place an empty metal bowl or cauldron. Have a piece of paper and pen nearby for writing.

Light the black candles, and say:

*All blocks are dissolved and burnt away.*
*Freedom to move comes to me today.*

Take a few moments to sit down and write all the negative things you want removed from your life, including any blockages. If you have a long list, it is better to use more than one small piece of paper, front and back, than to have difficulty getting a large paper into the cauldron. Don't worry if you miss something; you can repeat this ritual as many times as you need, but only once a week.

Fold your papers in half and return to stand before the altar. Light one paper at a time from one of the black candles. After it is burning good, drop it at a tilting angle into the cauldron. (The reason for the tilting angle is so all the paper will burn.) As you drop each burning paper into the cauldron, say:

*You are gone forever. You will never influence my*
*life again.*

Leave the candles to burn out. When the paper ashes and cauldron are cool enough, flush the ashes down the toilet.

# Conclusion

## A Note From the Author

It is perfectly permissible for magicians to write their own rituals once they fully understand the basics of magick and have enough sense to stay away from the dark side. If you insist on playing with magick on the dark side, you will eventually get your fingers burned severely. Do not blame this karmic repercussion on spells or magick if you were warned and stubbornly refused to listen! The fault will lie with you and no one or nothing else.

If you are a practicing Wiccan or Pagan, you may include the meditations and spells within your regularly cast circle. A properly cast circle adds to the power of both the spell and meditation.

# Other Reading Sources

Arrowsmith, Nancy, and George Moore. *A Field Guide to the Little People.* New York: Pocket Books, 1977.

Briggs, Katharine. An Encyclopedia of Fairies, Hobgoblins, Brownies, Bogies and Other Supernatural Creatures. New York: Pantheon Books, 1974.

Dance, S. Peter. *Shells.* New York: Dorling Kindersley, 1992.

Evans-Wentz, W. Y. *The Fairy Faith in Celtic Countries.* New York: Citadel Press, 1990.

Gachot, Theodore. *Mermaids: Nymphs of the Sea.* San Francisco, Calif.: HarperCollins, 1996.

Keightley, Thomas. *The World Guide to Gnomes, Fairies, Elves and Other Little People*. New York: Avenel Books, 1978. Originally published in 1880.

Mack, Carol K., and Dinah Mack. *A Field Guide to Demons, Fairies, Fallen Angels, and Other Subversive Spirits*. New York: Henry Holt and Co., 1998.

Page, Michael, and Robert Ingpen. *Encyclopedia of Things That Never Were*. New York: Viking, 1985.

Potts, Marc. *The Mythology of the Mermaid and Her Kin*. Chieveley, Berkshire: Capall Bann Publishing, 2000.

Osborne, Mary Pope. *Mermaid Tales from Around the World*. New York: Scholastic, Inc., 1993.

Rose, Carol. Spirits, Fairies, Leprechauns, and Goblins: An Encyclopedia. New York: W. W. Norton & Co., 1996.

Saxton, Patricia. *The Book of Mermaids*. North Charleston, S.C.: Booksurge, 2003.

Shaw, Eva. *Divining the Future*. New York: Gramercy Books, 1995.

# About the Author

A native of the Pacific Northwest, D.J. Conway (1939-2019) studied the esoteric and occult fields of spiritual practice for over 35 years. She authored over thirty books in the fields of magic, Wicca, Druidism, shamanism, metaphysics and the occult, and she authored of three fantasy novels. Born in Hood River, Oregon, to a family of Irish, North Germanic, and Native North American descent, she studied the occult and Pagan religion for over thirty years.

# To Our Readers

Weiser Books, an imprint of Red Wheel/Weiser, publishes books across the entire spectrum of occult, esoteric, speculative, and New Age subjects. Our mission is to publish quality books that will make a difference in people's lives without advocating any one particular path or field of study. We value the integrity, originality, and depth of knowledge of our authors.

Our readers are our most important resource, and we appreciate your input, suggestions, and ideas about what you would like to see published.

Visit our website at *www.redwheelweiser.com* to learn about our upcoming books and free downloads, and be sure to go to *www.redwheelweiser.com/newsletter* to sign up for newsletters and exclusive offers.

You can also contact us at *info@rwwbooks.com* or at

Red Wheel/Weiser, LLC
65 Parker Street, Suite 7
Newburyport, MA 01950